The Rose Avenue

Stories of Jewish Refugees in the Republic of San Marino During WWII

Stories of Jewish Refugees in the
Republic of San Marino During WWII

Author: Giuseppe Marzi
Copy Editor: Tiziano Thomas Dossena
Editors: Leonardo Campanile & Tiziano Thomas Dossena
Translation by: Maria Sara Forcellini & Lidia Ciolfi
Cover Design & Interior Layout: Dominic A. Campanile

Original title:
Il viale delle rose
Storie di ebrei rifugiati nella
Repubblica di San Marino
durante la seconda guerra mondiale

ISBN: ISBN: 978-1-948651-73-8
Library of Congress Control Number: 2026905227
Published by: Idea Press *(an imprint of Idea Graphics, LLC)* — Florida, USA
www.ideapress-usa.com • www.lideamagazine.com
Administrative Office, Florida, USA • email: ideapress33@gmail.com
Editorial Office, New York, USA • editoreusa@gmail.com

Printed in the USA - 1st Edition, March 7, 2026

GIUSEPPE MARZI

The Rose Avenue

Stories of Jewish Refugees in the Republic of San Marino During WWII

To the citizens of San Marino,
for their bravery and humanity.

"Although your dominion is small, your state is, nevertheless, one of the most honored in all history."

From a letter written on May 7, 1861
by U.S. President Abraham Lincoln
to the Republic of San Marino.

ACKNOWLEDGEMENTS

I searched many public and private archives, and many people have devoted their time, patience, understanding, and cooperation to my investigation. Some have given me their memories, others some documents, texts, and pictures, and still others their priceless experience.

I want to mention all those who have contributed to this work. Whether with small or large gestures, I thank them all:

Amedeo Montemaggi, Antonio Montanari, Franco Bonilauri, Shaul Ferrero, Giordano Reffi, Giuseppina Tamagnini, Roberto Tamagnini, Bruno Ghigi, Laura Rossi, Giorgio Zani, Gian Piero Gozi, Amalia Gozi, Manlio Gozi, Alceste Preda Ferri, Marisa Ferri, Marino Muccioli, Aroldo Casali, Renzo Bonelli, Marianna De Biagi, Maria José Mandelli, Noemi Ugolini, Ercole Gardini, Lorella Stefanelli, Elettra Zannini, Rosanna Pruccoli, Paolo Forcellini, Filippo Hill, Edoardo Brambilla Grimberg, Michael Gasperoni, Giovanni Michelotti, Giulio Caramaschi, Adelia Cesari, Liliana Picciotto Fargion, Michele Sarfatti, Laura Brazzo, Isa Corinaldi De Benedetti, Fabio Pedini Amati, Domenico Venturini, Michele Conti, Carl Fredric Marino Gumpert, Italo Scaramucci, Antonio Prioli, Giuseppe Renzi, Rosolino Martelli, Marco Casali, Giovanni Righi, Sandro Liberti, Lina Giannini, Paola Bigi, Federica Bigi, Sergio Nanni, Rav Stefano di Mauro, Rav Riccardo Di Segni, Massimo Lo Monaco, Annamaria Sirotti, Nicoletta Venturini, Maria Lea Pedini, Loredana Mazza, Carla Nicolini, Lenka Matusicova, Fernando Bindi, Simone Rafael Emdin, Elisabeth Klamper, Estee Yaari, Manuel Zonzini, Sergio Nanni, Natti Costantino, Otto Rühl, Augusto Stacchini, Vittorio Giardi, Ercole Giardi, Filippo Pruccoli, Don Giuseppe Innocentini, Gian Nicola Berti.

Of course, a special thank you goes to the person who patiently waited for my return from each interview — my wife, Azadeh.

PROLOGUE

— by Luciano Meir Caro —

Head Rabbi of the city of Ferrara and the Romagna region.

I have often wondered what happened to the Jews living in San Marino during World War II.

From an almost chance meeting that took place in the oldest Republic in the world, I discovered that Giuseppe Marzi had been dealing with this issue for some time, conducting research in various parts of the world with enthusiasm and, not without difficulty, through investigations, interviews, and much more.

The result of this research is the topic of this work, which was published in January 2012 and is now in its second edition due to the well-deserved success it has achieved.

For a long time, people have been discussing which suitable tools should be used to combat every form of hatred against "the Other." This hatred often leads to acts of discrimination against individuals or groups with specific values they do not want to relinquish. For centuries, Jews have served as emblematic evidence of a minority group subjected to various forms of oppression.

In the description of the events related to the Holocaust, the case of San Marino gains particular relevance due to this well-documented and easy-to-read book. It is a significant piece of the vast literature addressing this tragedy, which involved millions of people overwhelmed by an appalling escalation of violence.

The author documents how this welcoming Republic provided refuge to a significant number of Jews who consequently escaped a terrible fate. In the past, San Marino had already hosted a small group of Jews, who had little influence on this minor Republic, even though some of them had held institutional positions.

We do not know much about the events that followed. It turns out that many Jews sought refuge in San Marino during World War II, yet very little was known about this.

Starting from the evidence proving that, in 1944, the Government Offices of the Republic of San Marino issued a significant number of passports, Marzi began detailed research that led to the conclusion that such documents were issued to Jews seeking a way out of persecution. This occurred with the complicity of local authorities who, as is well known, held Fascist views. Of course, even the Italian members of the Fascist Party were aware of this situation but primarily chose to ignore it. As a result, dozens of people were saved.

This work is the ideal continuation of the research conducted by Amy Bernardy in the book called The Jews in the Republic of San Marino, published in 1904. There, she traced the history of the Jewish presence in San Marino up to the 17th century. Primarily engaged in mortgage banking and brokerage, the Jews were recognized for their ability to provide essential credit services to both private and public entities.

Many Jews were settled in villages and cities in the Marche and Emilia Romagna regions to engage in these activities. They were often invited by local governors, who recognized their usefulness. A similar situation occurred in San Marino, where, at the request of the Captains Regent (Heads of State), bankers and moneylenders arrived from Ancona, Rimini, and other cities.

The relationship with the local people was not always friendly. Sometimes, the Jews suffered acts of oppression and hostility, as occurred almost everywhere.

Giuseppe Marzi's investigation, which widens the scene of the relationship between San Marino and the Jews, was carried out with remarkable emotional involvement, and it urges researchers to continue in this direction.

This text makes a modest yet significant educational contribution by highlighting that this small state, the only one in Europe, faced great pressure from abroad and was not free from dangers, yet did not engage in acts of violence against these innocent people. Instead, it offered them refuge and protection, successfully avoiding the perversions of racism even during difficult times.

This is a valid lesson for all times, especially for our society, which seems to stray from the principles of dignity and justice that are so often professed yet frequently unheeded and ignored.

INTRODUCTION

— by Giuseppe Marzi —

San Marino is the only country in the world that behaved in a civilized way during World War II.

— **Prof. Amedeo Montemaggi**

This research began in 2000. In the past, while working for the State Television of the Republic of San Marino, I had covered dozens of news stories about the Second World War, the history of the Gothic Line, the one hundred thousand refugees who fled to San Marino to escape the war, the June 26, 1944 bombing and testimonies of all kinds. However, apart from the story of Ezio Giorgetti,[1] a hotel owner from Bellaria, I had never dealt with the Jewish issue.

But one fine day, a news story struck me like a lightning bolt. I was at the San Marino Museum of the Emigrant, a place that honors all the sacrifices made by the people of San Marino who endured starvation, power abuse, and various forms of exploitation to survive. They had left to seek their fortune elsewhere, as the world's oldest republic could not provide them with food in those days. On the entrance wall, I noticed a chart illustrating the evolution of passport issuance throughout the history of this small country of emigration.

What immediately caught my eye was the year 1944. While all the other years were marked by wooden sticks measuring no more than 30-35 centimeters, the one referring to that year almost reached the ceiling. I asked the director for further information, and she began

1. About Ezio Giorgetti see *Un cammino lungo un anno* (A year-long way) by Emilio Drudi, Giuntina ed.

to explain that there had been a surge of requests during that period because many citizens, frightened by the war, decided to flee. This struck me as rather odd, considering that the war did not affect San Marino, a neutral state. In fact, many people living nearby chose to take refuge there. However, she continued explaining that a significant portion of those documents had been falsified to allow Jews to escape from racial persecution. Although this information had become a sort of urban legend for them, it truly piqued my curiosity. At that point, I decided to investigate whether the story was true or not.

After some time and many unanswered questions, I returned to the museum and asked the director for more detailed information. Noemi Ugolini explained that she had checked the lists of passports issued between 1923 and 1962: "Yes, because before 1923 passports didn't exist. There was only an expatriation paper with a picture on it if the person had one; otherwise, it wasn't mandatory. Passports were introduced, however, in 1923. In order to get one, a citizen had to submit a specific application that was kept in the list of issued passports until the passport was returned. When the passport was no longer used or a request for renewal was made, the expired passport was then withdrawn and stored in the same list."

"It did occur," continued Mrs. Ugolini, *"that some people migrated and never returned to San Marino. In that case, they obtained a new nationality. So, if they had needed a passport, they would have gotten it from their new homeland. Either way, their original application would still be here in San Marino! Do you understand? There had to be either an application or a passport on the list! 12,000 passports were issued between 1923 and 1962, and there were only 11,200 passports returned or submitted applications that remained open! Then, we checked the names of those passport holders at the Registry. There, we found out that those people had never existed in San Marino! Or even better, their last names were all typical ones of the area, but not their first names, and their places of birth! They were all fake!'*

"Okay, but last time you talked about 500 passports, but when it comes to math, 12,000 minus 11,200 is 800! Do you mean that they increased in the meantime?"

"No, you must keep in mind that this story has moved from one public office to another for decades, just like a ghost would in a haunted castle. Maria Antonietta Bonelli, a historian, was the first person to deal with this case. I know for sure that in the sixties she thought that 500 of these passports had been given to the Jews and the remaining 300 to some deserters. This was done to allow the former to avoid racial persecution and the latter the war, do you understand? But she said it was just her deduction, there was no evidence, because nobody really knew where those passports ended up! This story seemed to die off there, at least until the day we decided to make that big chart on that wall over there on the trend of passport issuing in this country. 1944 really stands out... just look at how it shoots up."

While leaving, I stopped in front of the chart for a moment. I had seen it before, but this time it impressed me more. I reflected on how those vertical and parallel indicators, those numbers, represented human beings, their hardships, and power abuse. I thought about the plight of people fleeing hunger and ending up in the coal mines of Belgium or on the plantations of South America. Then, as I stared at the 1944 indicator, the images in black and white from Schindler's List came to mind. It was then that I decided, once and for all, that if that story were true, even if only in part, it absolutely had to be told. I continued my research by asking two questions: what risks would people face in San Marino — given that a Fascist government also existed here — if they helped the Jews? And moreover, if Maria Antonietta Bonelli had already investigated and found nothing, what could I possibly discover?

The issue "Jews in San Marino" had probably never been studied thoroughly before. If something like that had actually occurred, then surely every trace would have been canceled, or better yet, no trace was ever meant to exist.

I began to think about how so many passports could have been produced in a country like this. At that time, there were about 15,000 inhabitants. Therefore, the total of 800 passports, besides being a very high percentage for such a small population, could certainly not go unnoticed. Could a corrupt employee doing big business for himself have been involved in all this? It would have been a suicide attempt! Everyone knew each other in this place. The officials would have noticed it in the blink of an eye unless, of course, they were the ones doing it! "But no, it can't be true," I said to myself, "they were all full-fledged Fascists!" And they were all friends of Mussolini, who often came to San Marino for his romantic escapades with his mistress Claretta Petacci. No, it's out of the question!

The 17th-century Statutes include a specific oath for the Jews, indicating they also held institutional offices.[2] Additionally, we should note that two small Jewish communities had settled in this small Republic in the past. However, by the first half of the 19th century, almost all the members had either left or, rather, were driven away, as was periodically the case in other places as well. Two families, however, did remain, but they eventually converted to Catholicism. One of these families was the Bologna family, which is still present in the area.

I was told that in the first half of the last century, there was only one woman living in the ghetto. Her name was Gertrude. She was not Jewish, and the local girls would go to her house to learn how to sew men's clothing. She was the last person to live in what is still remembered today as the "Jewish ghetto."

She died around 1940, and since then, nobody seems to have returned to that place.

I continued to ask questions about those passports for a long time, inquiring of everyone I encountered. I wrote, seeking information from all around the world. I attempted to understand which routes were preferred at that time to escape a burning Europe. I posed questions in all these places, but no one had ever seen a single San Marino passport. Yet, when someone sees a foreign passport with this coat of arms stamped on it, they usually remember it very well. I recall,

---

2. *Statuta Decreta ac Ordinamenta illustris Republicae ac Perpetuae Libertatis Terrae Sancti Marini*, Giovanni Simbeni tip., Rimini 1600.

for instance, a few years ago at the airport in Tehran when I handed my passport to a border official. He grabbed it, left his post, and, screaming with happiness, ran all around the terminal showing it off to his colleagues. It was the first time he had seen one: it was as if he had won the lottery.

Every so often, someone would answer, "I heard about a Jew who was hiding there," and another would say, "I knew about a Jewish family hiding there," but no one had ever heard talk about passports. In books covering the local history, you can often read that "some Jews were also put up here," but nothing more.

Yad Vashem in Jerusalem was completely unaware of these passports, but their response made me even more anxious to continue my research after encountering so many dead ends. They had rekindled my spirit of challenge, which was slowly dwindling after such a long time. In response to my request for information about whether there was anything in their archives proving that San Marino had helped the Jews, they replied, "San Marino gave no help to Jews. There is only a photocopy of a document in our archives concerning San Marino, and it covers the law on the preservation of the Aryan race, which prohibited the marriage between people of different races, dated 1942. We found it in the archives in Berlin."[3]

That law, passed at the end of 1942, was undoubtedly late compared to other acts of persecution implemented throughout Europe. If it had been approved, I repeat, in that year and without reference to racial manifestos or prohibitions against and oppression of the Jews, there would surely have been a strong reason or considerable pressure from an external source. However, it must be emphasized that it served its purpose, as San Marino was also included in the list of countries collaborating with the Holocaust.

Then, one day, there was a change in direction! The father of a co-worker suggested I speak to one of his uncles. He was the son of the former Secretary of the San Marino Fascist Party and the nephew

---

3. Shaul Ferrero, superintendent of Yad Vashem Archives, Jerusalem.

of Giuliano Gozi, the undisputed Fascist leader in San Marino. This elderly man, who identified himself as a professional "grandfather," briefly mentioned that he knew his family had helped the Jews during World War II. He was willing to discuss it, but not that day because he had an urgent engagement with his grandchildren. So, he scheduled a meeting for the following week at his home. At first, I did not give much thought to the episode, but then, upon reflection, I changed my mind. This person had a vague awareness of some of the Jews, just like many others throughout the country; however, in this case, we were dealing with a member of a prominent Fascist family, those who were tasked with hunting down the Jews.

Yet that day he told me they had protected some of them. Although this strayed from the topic of the research I was conducting, it needed to be examined in depth.

A week later, I showed up on time at Gian Piero Gozi's house. There were two incredible surprises waiting for me there: the first was in his hand, the second in his head. Gozi handed me an envelope he had found in his family's archives. He said, "*Take a look at this.*" He allowed me to read a manuscript memorial written by his uncle Celio Gozi, a music teacher, shortly before his death. He was the only one in the family who had little to do with politics, yet he was still indirectly involved because of his brothers. Celio Gozi, in fact, recorded his recollections in an old, semi-rigid cardboard-covered account book whose spine was reinforced with masking tape. He titled it Memorial about the Jews in San Marino during the recent conflict. It was kept in a reused envelope labeled "JEWS 1981." His nephew, Gian Piero, had never seen the contents of that envelope, but knowing that I was searching for information on the Jews, he opened it, read its contents, and then painstakingly showed me the incredible discovery.

The text began by saying, "Many Italian and foreign Jews took refuge in San Marino during the Second World War to escape the persecution imposed by the Italian Kingdom and the Nazis. Everything was carried out respecting the century-old tradition of hospitality that this small Republic had always offered to the persecuted people of all nationalities." Then, he went on to state that, even though many years had passed since that time, people were still reticent, almost annoyed, about talking of the aid offered to the Jews, as if they were still risking reprisals by the Nazis for having helped them.

Celio Gozi seemed certain of one thing: there were a large number of Jews who took refuge in San Marino, but most of them could not be traced. He stated that even though our country had been identified as a Fascist Republic, the local government did not behave like the nearby Italians towards the Jews. He then went on to say what good people those Fascists had been — of course, because they were all his brothers. He provided an example: one day, while he was in his brother Giuliano's office, but his actual words were "at the Secretariat of State for Foreign Affairs with the Secretary of State, Attorney Giuliano Gozi" (this made me smile, considering the family relationship between the two, but I did not dwell much on such details), a group of Jews came in, introducing themselves to Giuliano Gozi as "Jews" and asked permission to settle down in San Marino. According to his brother, he replied: "Stay as long as you like in our warm-welcoming Republic," but advised them to be very discreet so that both the country and the Fascist government would not have any problems with either their neighbor, Italy, or the nearby German command.

He also believed that the government of Rome and the leaders of the Italian Fascist Party were well aware of the presence of Jews in San Marino but turned a blind eye to it. The local authorities in the nearby town of Rimini, as well as the Consul of Italy, Vincenzo Guglielmi, who was often in San Marino, also did not report it to his government.

Aside from the clear nostalgia for the Fascist period, which was so dear to him and his beloved brothers — I believe, in fact, that he was the last of the five still surviving — Gozi stated something that was absolutely true: namely, that the people in San Marino had a clear perception of the risk they were taking when they offered the Jews hospitality and shelter. At that point, I recalled the reply received from Yad Vashem in Jerusalem.

I was holding on to a text that argued the perspective in Israel about San Marino was the exact opposite of what Celio Gozi stated. On page five, his story continues: "Looking back at things, it can be said that the Fascist Republic of San Marino was the only country and the only Axis-controlled state in Europe which dared to welcome and protect Jews during the Second World War."

Then, he pointed out that the lack of names and personal details about most of those people was due to their great fear of being recognized and subsequently reported to the authorities. However, he underlined, "of the neighboring Italian towns", not to the authorities of San Marino! The Jews were always very discreet. At times, even the owners of the houses where they were staying were not aware of their true identity. He continued with the list of people he had known personally in those years who, according to him, were Jewish. He wrote down their names and provided some details about their lives and the houses where they sought refuge.

That text was undoubtedly important, but it contained no references to any documents. What he had written provided no evidence. It was his word against the entire world, which believed the exact opposite. I would need to check every syllable of that manuscript. Moreover, this was likely an extreme attempt to rehabilitate the memory of his brothers. After the war, in fact, they were convicted, imprisoned, and subsequently exiled from San Marino.

It should also be noted that if the allegations made by Celio Gozi were true, San Marino would have faced significant risks for providing the Jews with such alleged protection. It is impossible to calculate this with precision: there was no SS protocol that established the punishment for an entire country concealing Jews. Certainly, we are aware of cases where individuals who assisted some Jews were executed; we understand that there was no possibility of defense in this country, as there were neither weapons nor soldiers: the SS could have gulped down San Marino in a single swallow. It should be noted that on the island of Rhodes, the Italian soldiers who attempted to oppose the deportation of Jews were shot on the spot by the Nazis. In another instance, history tells us that Captain Lucente, the officer in charge of assessing Jewish property in southern Italy, buried the list he had created to prevent it from falling into Nazi hands. He received two death sentences, one from the Fascists and the other from the Nazis. By sheer luck in both instances, his life was spared.[4]

The second surprise I received from Gian Piero Gozi that day was incredible, at least as astonishing as the first one. Many times, I had spoken with the local elders about the Second World War, but never, until that moment, had I realized something truly extraordinary.

After I asked him to tell me where he was at the precise moment the bombs began to fall on June 26, 1944, I realized that his memories were suddenly regaining color: from a faded gray at the beginning, shapes and details of all kinds were suddenly reappearing. That wound, in the eyes of a man who had lived through that tragic period, had never really healed.

Only on that day did I realize that when, in the past, I had asked other elders to talk about that period, even those witnesses had behaved the same way. But now I could finally see the key to continuing my research. Gian Piero began to talk about the party he had attended the night before the bombing. He described the people he had met and the man from the stationery store who sold him games with a payment plan. Although the memories were not in perfect chronological order, the pictures I perceived were amazing and full of details.

At that point, I decided to talk to all the elders who had lived through that period of time, starting from that zero hour, exactly from that moment. Now, I could travel through a time I had never seen in person because I had others who had experienced it in my place. I must admit that in several cases, the awakening of those tragic recollections was almost an act of violence. Several people wept, while fear caused others to see things that had never existed in reality, such as low-flying fighter planes strafing the streets of the old town center. This had

---

4. Gregorio Caravita, *Ebrei in Romagna (1938-1945) dalle leggi razziali allo sterminio* (Jews in the Romagna region (1938-1945) from Racial Laws to extermination), Longo ed., Ravenna.

never actually taken place. Yet, some people were genuinely convinced they had seen them and heard the shots on the people in the streets. However, I must say that these mirages had only been seen on June 26th, that fearful day.

Giordano Reffi told me during his recollections: "*The most difficult task in San Marino during the war was to organize dinner and dance parties.*"[5] Entering the war so suddenly was traumatic for everyone. In order to see the war up to that time, they had to climb up to the top of Mount Titano and look towards the horizon. However, the war, that day, took them by surprise and came for no apparent reason.

I soon realized that when I posed specific questions about people and places from that period to those who had lived through those moments, I received vivid images from various perspectives. It was like having multiple cameras converging from different angles toward a single target: they provided me with a three-dimensional view of what I wanted to see.

I interviewed many witnesses, but the person who impressed me most was one woman in particular. Her name is Giuseppina Tamagnini, but I nicknamed her my "time machine." She was a child at the time, but she has always had the great gift of observation. I would wind her up as you would a model car, then I would give her the name of a person and launch her back to 1944. She would suddenly come back with an astonishing description: how tall the person was, his way of speaking, what he said, what he dressed like, even how he wore his hair!

Initially, I could hardly believe it; however, I soon realized that when I asked other people about the same individual mentioned by Tamagnini, they sometimes didn't even know who they were. But when I provided them with the visual description from my "time machine," everything suddenly clicked back into place, and they confirmed the image, adding more details. One of the many stories she shared with me, remarkable in its visual description, was about a woman who came to San Marino from Rimini to buy meat:

---

5. From the interview with Giordano Reffi, RSM.

"Many people came to shop up here," she said, *"one day I was on a train waiting to depart. We were going to the beach. At some point, the police got on the train and started to check everyone. A big woman next to me pulled out a huge hunk of meat from under her dress. To avoid giving it to the police, she decided to throw it out of the window, exclaiming: "A no questa in la tò [No, they won't get this]." She threw the meat, but the train window was closed, so it stuck to the glass for a few seconds and then slowly slid onto the floor. I'll never forget the look of amazement on that lady's face and all the people's laughter. Then, the police approached her, sending us children away first. I don't know what they did to her."*[6]

The fact that people came to buy meat in San Marino was also confirmed by Bruno Chigi, a publisher from Rimini: *"I used to go up there too because the meat was better and costed less."*[7]

Then she told me about a Jewish woman from Rimini. Her mother would occasionally go to her apartment in the Bellariva area and bring her food: "Her last name was Neri. My mom's cousin, who lived nearby, had asked us if we could occasionally bring her things to eat because she was always locked up in her house."[8]

At that point, I had a text that, although important, could only serve as an outline. However, I also had several witnesses who could confirm whether what Celio Gozi had seen was true or not.

From that day on, memories filled with names began to fall from the sky like snowflakes. Along with the names came documents, photographs, and letters that led me to other names and additional documents.

Even from the archives, where I had previously been told that there was nothing concerning the Jews in San Marino, new references now revealed everything. I recorded and transcribed every syllable of what I was told by the witnesses. Each piece was like a crucial part of a vast jigsaw puzzle, being assembled before my eyes. I was

6. From the interview with Giuseppina Tamagnini, RSM.

7. From the interview with Bruno Ghigi, Rimini.

8. From the interview with Giuseppina Tamagnini, RSM.

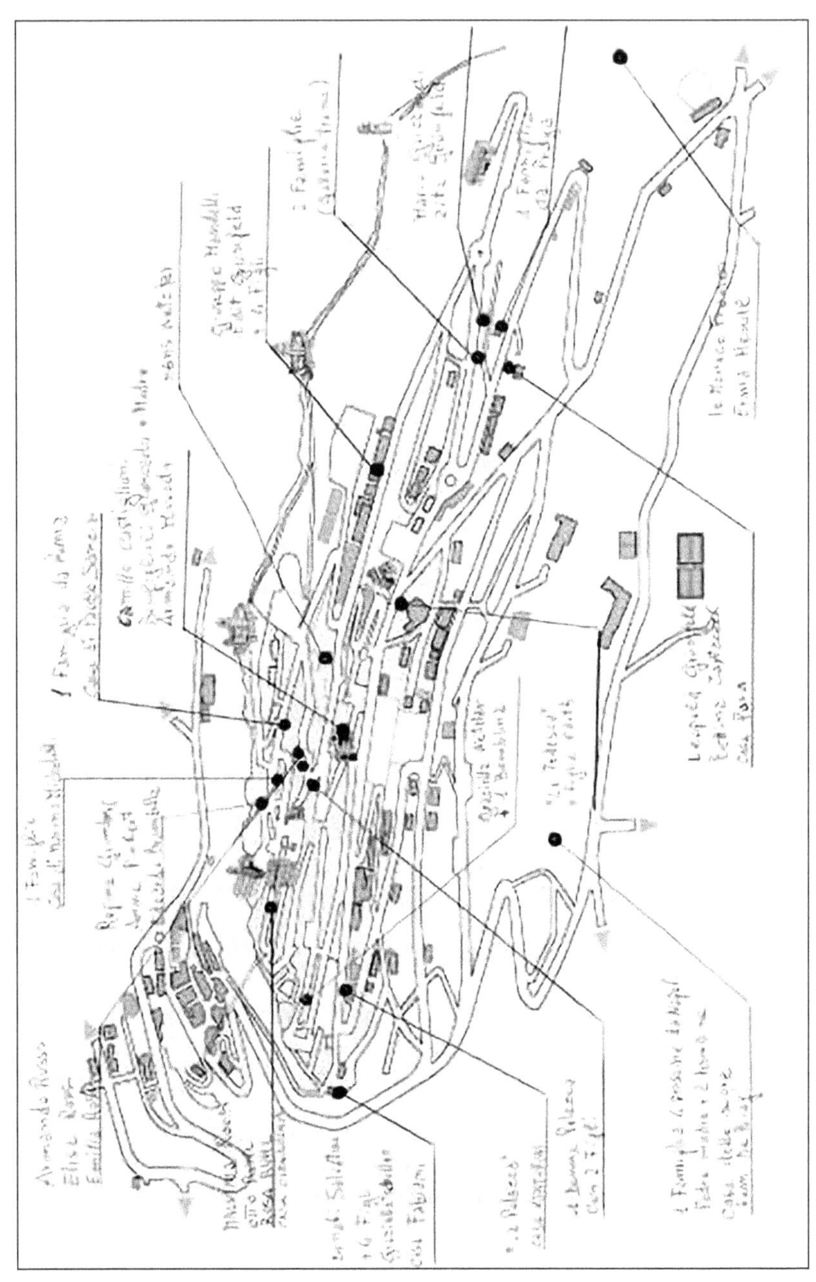

The map of San Marino Città with the indication of the Jews who lived there during the Second World War, according to the memories collected.

reconstructing a story that had never been told before. My first step was to take a map of the old town center of San Marino and mark all the houses where the presence of Jewish families had been indicated, even if just assumed. The resulting image was impressive. It became clear that a Jewish concentration of this size in such a small place could not have gone unnoticed by the pro-Nazi authorities. Either those rulers pretended to be pro-Nazi, or another hypothesis could be that they acted as Fascists only when it came to punishing those who did not wear a black shirt, but nonetheless, they were not racists!

I realized, too many years later, that I was looking for something that had not been filed away on some dusty shelf but was locked up in the memory of those men and women who, more than sixty-six years ago, had seen their faces, heard their voices, and actually talked to them.

In some cases, they did not even know their real names; in other cases, they did not even know their fake ones. However, step by step, all the pieces were coming together. One person knew a name, another a last name, and then the origin. Eventually, I would find a friend or family member still living who would tell me the whole story and provide some written proof showing me that what I had been told was true.

Therefore, this is not merely a simple historical investigation presenting only names, dates, and places; rather, it is the story of a significant number of Jews from various European countries who experienced the periods of Racial Laws and deportations, up to the end of the war in the Republic of San Marino. This narrative is primarily conveyed through the memories of those who witnessed and knew them personally, men and women who have also led me to discover several documents that partially rewrite the recent history of the world's oldest Republic.

Table of Contents

"ZERO HOUR"

The years of history seem long and far away. Actually, they are just a breath and the events apparently lost in that dimension of history that is time are close and linked to each other by that mysterious and strong thread which is men's memory.

— Andrea Rossi

The morning of June 26, 1944 – 30 minutes to Zero Hour (11:01 am)

The air was warm that morning on Mount Titano, the sky was clear, and the streets were crowded with people coming and going. There was a peaceful atmosphere all around in the old town. At the Public Palace a German officer was visiting; he was the head of the command of Mercatino Marecchia, today's Novafeltria.[9] He was there to meet the Captains Regent (Heads of State) Francesco Balsimelli and Sanzio Valentini, while all the other members of the Government, outside of that office, were trying to figure out what would happen soon after. Further south, the Gustav line had been broken through, and after the liberation of Rome, which took place 16 days earlier, the advance of the Allied troops would have no other obstacles up to the Gothic line.[10]

---

9. From the interview with Attorney Giorgio Zani, RSM.

10. Amedeo Montemaggi – Itinerari della Linea Gotica 1944. Guida storico iconografica ai campi di battaglia (Itineraries of the Gothic Line 1944. Historical-Iconographic guide of the battle fields) – 2010 ed. Museo dell'Aviazione – Rimini.

Yes, the Gothic Line, one of the longest trenches ever built, running through Italy from the Adriatic to the Tyrrhenian Seas and skirting the Republic of San Marino. For some time, the people on that patch of land had been getting ready for the worst: a company called the Border Militia had been trained quickly. It was a unit formed by about sixty young militiamen led by Colonel Alvaro Casali and Captain Federico Bigi. *"They all had diplomas or degrees, but they were all unemployed,"*[11] Lieutenant Giorgio Zani explained. They had at their disposal a total of six Beretta submachine guns. Marshal Rodolfo Graziani of the Italian Social Republic[12] had given them eight guns to be used by the local police unit, but the government decided to give only two to the police and the rest to the young soldiers who had sworn in the previous afternoon. That morning, they were all there taking orders and positions on the ground floor of Palazzo Begni, the headquarters of the Border Militia in those days.

The houses were packed with displaced people, and so were the twelve railway tunnels linking San Marino to Rimini. There were already more than 70,000 people, and more continued to arrive from the nearby Italian towns.

The groups were often headed by a priest holding a white flag. They were all seeking refuge in that small neutral territory.[13] Signs written in various languages had been hung up along the border. They warned the soldiers that they could not exceed that limit. Large white crosses had been drawn on the roofs of the houses and in the fields to remind the pilots not to release their bombs there.[14]

Giuseppina Tamagnini had left her house to go to the Parish church.[15] She was 11 years old, and school had finished for her

11. From the interview with Attorney Giorgio Zani, RSM.
12. State Archives of the Republic of San Marino, Ezio Balducci archive, letter dated 3 July 1944.
13. Amedeo Montemaggi, San Marino nella bufera: 1943–44: gli anni terribili (San Marino in the Storm: 1943-44: the Terrible Years), San Marino, Arti grafiche Della Balda, 1984.
14. From the interview with Attorney Giorgio Zani, RSM.
15. From the interview with Giuseppina Tamagnini, RSM.

the week before. On the other hand, Gian Piero Gozi, who was a year younger, still had lessons in the building that now houses the State Museum.[16] The teacher, Alceste Preda Ferri, had walked from Montegiardino to pick up her salary at the Public Palace.[17] Shortly before, Marino Muccioli had been hired by a truck driver to help him load 60 mattresses onto his truck. They were to be transported from the convent of Saint Francis to the border points where the Militia would settle down.[18]

Soldier Aroldo Casali had already received his orders from the headquarters, and as he was off duty for a few hours, he headed back to his home in Borgo Maggiore.[19] Giordano Reffi, instead, along with some other fellow soldiers, decided to stop at the café in the square, Piazza Titano, to have a last drink before carrying out the hard work he had as a Border Guard.[20] Renzo Bonelli was lying on his bed, reading a book;[21] Marianna De Biagi was with two little girls, the daughters of some displaced people, in her vegetable garden, picking some Swiss chards that she would cook later.[22] Maria José Mandelli, who everyone called "Baby", was on her way to meet Gina Zani. Together, they were going to the shoemaker at the end of the village to have something repaired.[23]

June 26, 1944 - 3 minutes to Zero Hour (11:28 am):

Lieutenant Giorgio Zani was dictating a letter addressed to the head of the department assigned to food stock control so that he could organize the rations for the soldiers who were getting ready to start

16. From the interview with Gian Piero Gozi, RSM.
17. From the interview with Alceste Preda Ferri, Cattolica.
18. From the interview with Marino Muccioli, RSM.
19. From the interview with Aroldo Casali, RSM.
20. From the interview with Giordano Reffi, RSM.
21. From the interview with Renzo Bonelli, RSM.
22. From the interview with Marianna De Biagi, RSM.
23. From the interview with Maria José Mandelli, Reggio Calabria.

their service at the borders. At the same time, a British reconnaissance aircraft was flying over San Marino at a medium-low altitude. Very few people paid any attention to it because Allied planes going to Rimini to drop their bombs had been flying for months in the sky

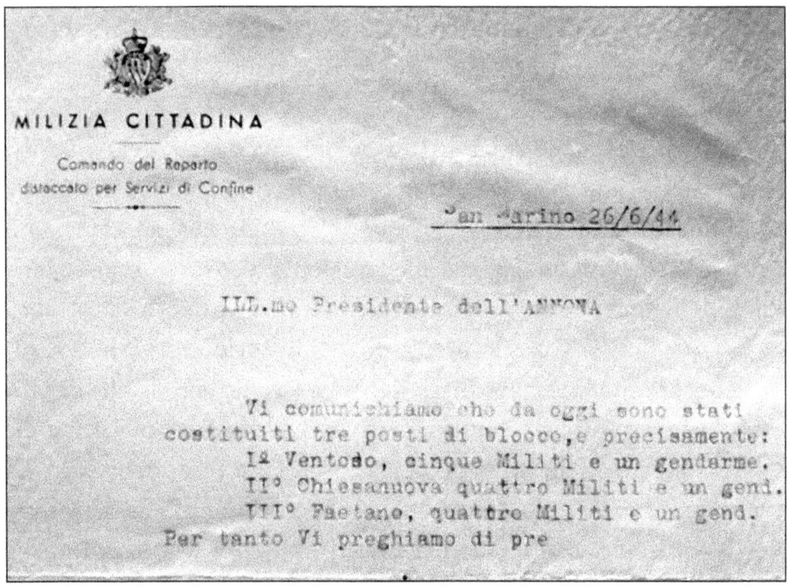

MILIZIA CITTADINA

Comando del Reparto
distaccato per Servizi di Confine

San Marino 26/6/44

ILL.mo Presidente dell'ANNONA

Vi comunichiamo che da oggi sono stati costituiti tre posti di blocco,e precisamente:
I° Ventoso, cinque Militi e un gendarme.
II° Chiesanuova quattro Militi e un gend.
III° Faetano, quattro Militi e un gend.
Per tanto Vi preghiamo di pre

Giorgio Zani's letter was interrupted when the first bomb exploded.
— Courtesy of Giorgio Zani's collection. —

STATE MILITIA
Headquarters of the Brigade
for Border Servicing

San Marino, 06/26/1944

To the president of the department assigned to food stock control

We inform you that three checkpoints have been established today, namely:

1st Ventoso, five soldiers and a policeman.

2nd Chiesanuova, four soldiers and a policeman.

3rd Faetano, four soldiers and a policeman.

Therefore, we ask you to pre...

over the small country. Some children, who were getting ready to leave the elementary school building, were watching from the window: after school, they used to go to the top of the mountain to see the bombings along the coast. They had understood that a reconnaissance aircraft always came before the bombers. It would fly over the area at a lower altitude and drop some red balloons.

They did not know exactly what those balloons were used for, but it was clearly a signal. They also saw the same signal at that moment.[24] This time, however, the balloons were not being dropped on the faraway coast, but right over the roof of their school. Scared to death, they began to scream. The teachers and janitors made them lie down under their desks and against the walls; no one was allowed out. A little higher up, Giuseppina Tamagnini, while walking down the steep road, heard some women saying, *"Hey ... Look at those balloons... who knows where they come from?"* Attorney Bellisardi looked up at the sky and started shouting at the top of his lungs, *"Get in a safe place... get down on the ground!"*[25] Everybody in Liberty Square lay down, hugging the nearby city walls. But she didn't. She remained standing, leaning against the wall of the restaurant "La Taverna". Sixty-six years later, she said, *"I heard an annoying whistle, like a high-screeching buzz. I leaned out and saw a big red bomb coming down, leaving a thin trail of black smoke behind."*

Republic of San Marino, June 26, 1944, 11:31 am, Zero Hour.

I read the list of names recorded in Gozi's memorial to Giuseppina Tamagnini. She knew almost every one of them. She said something under her breath, then lifted her head. She looked at me and said, *"But if those were Jews, then I knew others as well!... Even the German woman must have been Jewish!... Of course! If not, what else was she doing here?"*[26]

---

24. From the interview with Gian Piero Gozi, RSM.

25. From the interview with Giuseppina Tamagnini, RSM

26. From the interview with Giuseppina Tamagnini, RSM

1938
THE PROCLAMATION OF RACIAL LAWS

Even in San Marino, there was a Fascist government, just like in Italy. Giuliano Gozi, the fourth of Gemino Gozi's five children, was the stage director of that farce. He had inherited the title of Count from his father. Actually, five generations before, his great-grandfather Federico II had married Maria Virginia degli Oliva da Piagnano. Through this marriage, the Gozi family became a member of the noble elite of Urbino, or at least so it seems from the family tree drawn up in 1939. Giuliano III was born on August 7, 1894. He got his law degree in Bologna, where, in 1914, he also took part in the demonstrations in favor of Italy's entry into war. He returned to San Marino in May 1915, but only to recruit local volunteers. Then, he tried to enlist in the 27th Regiment of Forlì, but he was rejected, so he volunteered in the 35th Infantry Regiment of Bologna. He was accepted there and sent to the military school of Modena. In November 1915, Gozi reached the rank of Lieutenant and was immediately sent with the 3rd Alpine Troopers to the Boite valley, where he fought in the fierce battles along the Piave River line. On July 29, 1916, he was honored with the Gold Medal for military valor in the field with the following motivation: "*As a commander of an advanced guard platoon, he showed firmness and courage, lunging under the enemy's barbed wire to cut it, staying there for a long time despite the intense fire, and retreating only after receiving orders from his superior.*" Gozi had to leave the

Italian Royal Army on September 4, 1918, because he was appointed Secretary of State for Foreign Affairs in San Marino. For that reason, he refused to receive the medal for military valor for volunteer fighting.[27]

In 1922, Gozi founded the San Marino Fascist Party and placed all his relatives and most trusted friends in key positions. In March 1923, elections were held, and at that point, Giuliano Gozi's San Marino Fascist Party had no other political rival. He was appointed Captain Regent five times and had only one big thorn in his side, namely "Ezio Balducci".

Balducci was born in Serravalle on August 23, 1904. He graduated with honors in Medicine and Surgery from the University of Bologna. Then, he volunteered at the local pediatric clinic there. In 1930, Balducci commuted between San Marino and Bologna. He was elected Town Councilor in San Marino, while in Bologna, he was appointed Editor of the Fascist newspaper "L'Assalto" (The Assault), founded by the journalist Nanni Leone Castelli. This newspaper was famous because it criticized Mussolini's politics for being "too soft". Balducci was appointed Director after Leo Longanesi. He became Captain Regent during the period October 1, 1929 to April 1, 1930, but his political skills and, above all, his fame in San Marino frightened the Gozi family. Balducci had all the people living in the lower part of the town on his side, including the farmers who had always considered those living in the old town center as the privileged class who took advantage of them. In 1934, accused of plotting a coup d'état and making an attempt on the Captains Regent's lives, he was taken to trial. On March 26 of that year, Balducci was sentenced to 20 years of hard labor and then forced into exile along with his closest friends and collaborators. He did not give up hope, however, and had a brilliant career in Italy both as a politician and physician.[28]

---

27. Verter Casali, *Appunti di Storia* (History notes) in *Il Corriere Sammarinese*, Issue no. 45, Friday, May 14, 2004.

28. *Ezio Balducci, per non dimenticare* (Ezio Balducci, not to forget) – publication edited by Maria Lea Pedini, Director of Cultural Affairs and Information at the Secretariat of State for Foreign Affairs of the Republic of San Marino – 1996.

Giuliano Gozi.

On March 18, 1938, Balducci was informed by Ferruccio Martelli that Italo Balbo intended to mediate a reconciliation between him and Giuliano Gozi. The famous aviator was highly regarded in San Marino, having lived and studied there, but Balducci did not want to hear a thing about it and volunteered for the war in Africa, where he was honored with two medals for military valor. In January 1941, Balducci was declared missing in action, but they found out later that he had been wounded and taken prisoner by the British. He was able to make his way back to Italy only in April 1942, after an exchange of disabled prisoners.[29]

The presence of two Jewish women was the first to be noted immediately after the proclamation of the notorious "Racial Manifest".

For the people of San Marino, one of them was and always would be "the German". Hardly anyone knew her name, and most

29. Maria Alice Brusa – Degree thesis entitled: *Il ruolo di Ezio Balducci nel Fascismo italiano e sammarinese* (The role of Ezio Balducci in the Italian and San Marino Fascism) – 7th cycle of doctorate in History years 2005/2008 – University of the Republic of San Marino.

people would never know it. Only Ercole Gardini seemed to be better informed than the others: "*Her name was Carlotta.*"[30] Even though everyone used to see her around, they would notice her daughter, Edith, more than her. The people described the mother as a middle-aged woman as tenacious as a Neapolitan mastiff, while the daughter was the most beautiful girl to set foot in San Marino. At that time, all the boys were in love with her, but the blonde Edith was always accompanied by her mother, who never left her alone and was stuck to her like glue.

Then, there was another problem: shyness; then again, there was the language. Many people, in fact, thought she could only speak German, but she did not actually come from Germany. Giuseppina Tamagnini knew they had come from Milan, yet their real origin remained unknown. Ercole Gardini, however, argued that those three people had originally come down from Bolzano. Yes, three people. In the house bought by the Zavoli family, right below the Capuchin convent, a

Ezio Balducci; 1928.
(State Library of the Republic of San Marino.)

30. From the interview with Ercole Gardini, RSM.

man was also living with Carlotta and her daughter Edith. He was hardly ever seen around. This elderly man used to be a doctor. He was ill and constantly in need of assistance, so Carlotta was his nurse. Giordano Reffi said: *"I don't know how, but once those two coupled,"* and then he fondly added, *"That woman was against temptations. No one ever understood how she could have given birth to such a beautiful daughter!"*[31]

According to some witnesses, they arrived in San Marino shortly before the beginning of the war and remained there during the whole conflict. When they got there, the daughter must have been about 15 or 16 years old. *"As soon as he saw her"*, continued Reffi, *"my cousin Virginio began to study German so he could talk to her. He immediately dove into it. I remember that, when she was 18, she looked like a goddess... but not like today's models... she was much prettier."* Then he looked up to the sky and started daydreaming. *"Ah, she was so pretty... what a smile she had."*

Giuseppina Tamagnini remembered that she used to see them in those years when she went to steal some "visciole" — this is how black cherries are called around here — with other children. The tree was in their garden, *"where the Turismo movie theater is now located."*[32] Distracted by so much beauty, none of the boys at that time thought what could have been the reason those people had moved to a place that could offer nothing more than a nice view. The only thing that surprised the people of San Marino was that they never knew how they supported themselves. Where did they get the money they were living on? They were always so well dressed as well. Carlotta would often receive letters and would always tell the postman to give them directly to her. She would say: *"If I'm not at home, keep them and you can give them to me next time."*[33]

31. From the interview with Giordano Reffi, RSM.

32. From the interview with Giuseppina Tamagnini, RSM

33. From the interview with Giuseppina Tamagnini, RSM In the original text the woman speaks with a German accent and there are some grammar errors [Translator's note]

In San Marino, The Racial Manifest was never accepted, unlike all the other Fascist rules. It must be said that no acts of violence caused by racist reasons had ever been recorded, especially because here, during those years, there was no incitement to behave contemptuously against Jews, while it could easily happen in the nearby city of Rimini.

In the bottom right corner of this old picture is the house where Carlotta and her daughter, Edith, lived.
— Courtesy of the State Library of San Marino. —

These were probably the reasons why the two women could walk peacefully along the streets of the small Republic. It is not that ordinary people did not realize that they could have been Jewish; it was simply that for most of them, it was not at all a problem. The only big problem was for the young men who were desperately looking for the courage and the right strategy to approach the blonde, Edith. Yet, no one thought of asking her why they had moved to that place or even her name.

This was widely accepted in San Marino. When a person's name was not known, he or she would often be given a nickname that identified his or her presumed country of origin. This way, the local people could talk, or even better gossip, like in this case, about "the German" or the "German's daughter." This, we must underline, was not an isolated case.

Surely, there were other Jews in that period. For example, if you check the ossuaries of the cemetery of Montalbo, precisely the one where the people living in the higher part of the country were buried, there is a tomb with the following engraving on it: Erminia Levi Marchi, born in 1857, died in 1940. There seem to be no ties with the families of San Marino, not even her husband's name, Luigi Marchi, who had died two years earlier and had been buried next to her. When I asked for their death certificates, everyone at the Registry Office jumped out of their skin. Of course, it was not due to the request but to what was found. Those people's documents had been clearly falsified.[34] They were made not to be permanently false because the changes could be easily distinguished, and there were notes that, one day, would tell the truth were left behind. Someone had left a historical record that told how things had gone. But to discover the truth, you had to look for that document having a specific address and also have a clear awareness of what you were searching for.

Both Erminia and her husband Luigi were referred to as immigrants, but the year of their arrival in San Marino was missing. They probably went there in 1938 when Luigi died. The last name Levi was clearly changed into Livi, and she was the daughter of Antonio Levi, also transformed into Livi, and Maria Casagrande, which became Casadei. Incredibly, fake last names were quoted at the foot of the page next to the real names of those people.

According to the papers, after her husband's death, Erminia Levi married Luigi Tamagnini, a man from Borgo Maggiore. There was no wedding date indicated. Consequently, the ceremony was somewhat hasty since her first husband had died in 1938, and she died in 1940. Moreover, she became a widow at the age of 81. Either way,

34. Registry Office of the Republic of San Marino.

the Marchis did not come to San Marino alone. Their five children, Sofia, Giovanni, Adalcisa, Giuseppe and Iolanda, all from Turin and Florence, were also recorded at the Registry. Another strange situation for the time is that both Adalcisa and Iolanda were single, but each of them had a child whose fathers were indicated as "Unknown" on the papers at the San Marino Registry Office. Another oddity to be noticed on these documents is that one of these "fatherless" children had emigrated to Florence all alone at the tender age of seven. This all looked very suspicious to the office clerks and manager. Yet, suddenly, it became clear that those people were seeking refuge from the Italian Racial Laws. From the same papers, it transpired that all those people had left San Marino; all except one, Sofia Marchi, who married Michele Pignatta from San Marino and was finally included in the 1947 census.

In that same period, the arrival of three other people could be traced. Almost surely, this was also a case of a mixed marriage: a man named Franco Lo Monaco, his wife Erma Hendl, and her mother, who never had a name for the inhabitants of San Marino. She was simply referred to as "old Mrs. Hendl." The first trace of them could be found in Celio Gozi's writings. He wrote that the old lady lived in the house belonging to a nurse named Vio Cornacchia. Nobody had ever seen her outside the house, or rather, added Gozi, *"she was so afraid of being seen and recognized by the Germans that she had never even stuck her nose out of the window!"*[35] Her daughter and son-in-law lived in a house located in the place called "I fondi del Voltone" (Voltone plots), more or less where the clay shooting ground now lies. Lo Monaco was born in the province of Siracusa and, according to Gozi, was a goldsmith. However, the rabbi of Siracusa, Stefano Di Mauro, denied that this name resulted from the local Jewish archives. Therefore, it can be assumed that only his wife was from there.

But the information was really scarce then, so to find some confirmation, I went where, according to Gozi, they used to live before

35. Celio Gozi, *Memoria sugli Ebrei a San Marino durante l'ultimo conflitto* (Memorial about the Jews in San Marino during the recent conflict) – Gozi's Collection, RSM.

they took refuge in San Marino, that is, the house on Via Trento 2 in Rimini. However, no one there seemed to have heard of that name. The employees of the local Registry Office kindly repeated the search several times, but nothing came out in regard to Franco Lo Monaco and Erma Hendl. I went back to the building on Via Trento. Once again, I spoke to all the elders I met in the street, but nothing. Then, I reached the newsstand in the nearby square and asked the owner how long it had been there. She told me that she had been running that business for 20 years, but before her, there was another woman who had been there for decades. She told me the woman's name and the street where she lived. I went there and started asking questions about the old newsstand owner. She finally appeared, and I asked the same old question: "Do you know who lived in that house?" She said she did not remember, but there was a florist nearby who would remember. Finally, she told me who I had to talk to in order to have certain information about that building: the person I had to look for was Elettra Zannini.

Mrs. Zannini affirmed that the building had always been there. She moved in there in 1964, but before that, it belonged to her mother-in-law, who had told her about the war days many times. "*She owned several apartments in this building and rented them to tourists. During the war, she had several families as guests, but I don't remember that last name, Lo Monaco. When the bombings started, she made them all run away. The son of one of those families died during those days. He was a young boy. He was buried in my husband's family tomb, and he's still there today.*"[36]

The small building on Via Trento 2 is located in the heart of the beach area of Rimini, right in front of the most historic bathing establishment: the "Neptune". It must be remembered that at that time there were several cases of Jews pretending to be tourists on holiday. This is the case of the 37 Jews of Croatian origin who took shelter in Ezio Giorgetti's hotel in Bellaria. He also obtained fake documents for them. Or the case of Cesare Moisè Finzi, who, in

36. From the interview with Elettra Zannini, Rimini.

his autobiography *Qualcuno si è salvato* (Someone was saved) talks about the ups and downs he experienced in the hotels and guesthouses of Gabicce, before taking refuge in Valconca.

Many people took advantage of the fact that on the Adriatic coast there was a myriad of hotels and guesthouses in which they could find shelter. The episode told by Mrs. Zannini makes way for some thought: one of the guests was killed by a bomb, but the bombing over Rimini began on November 1, 1943. Rimini was usually deserted in November. So, what kind of tourists were they? The woman did remember some last names, and bingo! — most of them were typically Jewish.

So, we can assume that Franco Lo Monaco was a Catholic, but he had married a Jew, Erma Hendl, and with his wife's mother, he escaped persecution by hiding in the house of Mrs. Zannini's mother-in-law. She was willing to accommodate them taking turns with other Jews, but due to the increasing risk and to avoid arousing suspicion, she made them flee to safer areas. Perhaps, she herself sent Lo Monaco to someone she knew in San Marino. Many people from San Marino used to walk along that street at the time because it linked the train station to the beach. It might have been a member of the Gozi family. In fact, Celio Gozi seemed to be the only one who knew the age of the old woman: "*She was about 80 years old,*" he said.

So far, these are the stories of the witnesses. The reality derived from the documents indicated, however, that the "Lo Monaco" family arrived in San Marino from Merano, in the province of Bolzano,[37] exactly on October 4, 1939.[38] Franco Lo Monaco, an accountant, was born on November 8, 1892, in Florida, in the province of Siracusa. His wife, Erma Hendl, was born on November 2, 1894, in Vienna. Her father's name was Bertoldo; he had probably already died by that time. The name of "old Mrs. Hendl", hidden in Cornacchia's house, was Malvina Kohn, and she too, like her daughter, was from Vienna, but of German nationality. They were sent away from the city of

37. Jewish Museum of Merano, kind courtesy of Rosanna Pruccoli.

38. Registry Office of the Republic of San Marino.

Merano in July 1939, so it was likely they moved first to Via Trento 2 in Rimini and then to San Marino on October 4 of that same year.

This is the date filed at the San Marino Registry. At this point, it can also be assumed that those people also knew Carlotta, whom everyone called "the German". She was originally from a small village a few kilometers from Merano, so they could have decided to come to San Marino together.

A further confirmation came from Rosanna Pruccoli, head of the Jewish Museum in Merano: Erma Hendl Lo Monaco and Malvina Kohn Hendl, class of 1870, were recorded as members of the Jewish community of Merano, and they were still there according to the 1938 Fascist census. Pruccoli also explained that after that census, 500 Jews of foreign nationality were sent away from Merano. Among them was also Malvina Kohn, the "old Mrs. Hendl." Pruccoli pointed out that in several cases, those people moved in small groups or often went to places already explored by others of the same religion. Consequently, their relationship with Carlotta, "the German," can once again be assumed.

It must be said that the members of a Fascist government, even in a small town, must be aware of the origins of those people, given the public security control policy in force. They were dictators. However, it should be noted that the Jews were never expelled from San Marino. During the Fascist period, expulsion was used only against citizens of San Marino accused of anti-fascist activities or, at least, against those who tried to usurp Gozi's power.

Further evidence that local Fascists did not apply any racial rules, as the Italians did instead, is a recollection of Professor Carla Nicolini, daughter of Giuseppe Nicolini, who was at that time the representative in San Marino of the large international insurance company Generali and a close friend of Giuliano Gozi. *"One day, shortly after the proclamation of Racial Laws in Italy,"* said Ms. Nicolini, *"Marco Ara, top executive of Generali, who lived in Venice, came to see my father with a suitcase in hand and asked him if he could safeguard it in San Marino. It was full of gold bars. My father did not feel like keeping it in our*

Via Giovan Battista Belluzzi; the house on the left with the open shutters was indicated as Vio Cornacchia's home. Above the arch in the foreground lived the fascist leader Giuliano Gozi.

home, so he took Ara to Giuliano Gozi and asked him to hide the suitcase in his house. He accepted."[39]

Marco Ara was a cousin of Edgardo Morpurgo, the chairman of Generali. They were the sons of sisters Carolina and Rosina Levi. They were Jews of ancient lineage, and along with their family, they held the majority share of Generali Insurance. Before the Racial Laws in 1938, Morpurgo was forced to cede the presidency to Gino Baroncini, a man highly regarded by Benito Mussolini. By doing so, at least formally, the Morpurgo family was removed from the leadership of this insurance giant. Moreover, Generali also lost all its branches in the Eastern European countries already occupied by the Nazis.[40]

While the hunt for Jews was intensifying across Europe, San Marino, a small strip of land in the heart of Mussolini's Italy, began to provide shelter to sporadic and discreet Israelites. The local Fascists not only turned a blind eye to this but, as in the case of Marco Ara's gold, even collaborated with them.

In that period, another man arrived in the heart of the old town center of San Marino. From Ancona came Armando Russi, born in 1894 and son of Giuseppe Russi, who had been appointed Consul of San Marino in Ancona in 1921. His family had lived in the capital of the Marche region, first on Via San Martino, then in Piazza Cavour 8, and finally, on Corso Vittorio Emanuele 13, at least up to 1939 when Giuseppe Russi died and was buried in the local Jewish cemetery.[41]

Armando Russi had a degree in Social Sciences; he had studied the piano and graduated from the Rossini Conservatory in Pesaro, under the guidance of Maestro Amilcare Zanella.

This passion allowed him to share some time with Celio Gozi, who described him as "*a pianist of a certain prestige*". In the past, the

39. From the interview with Carla Nicolini, RSM.

40. Anna Millo – *Trieste, le Assicurazioni, L'Europa – Arnoldo Frigessi di Rattalma e la RAS* (Trieste, insurance companies, Europe – Arnoldo Frigessi of Rattalma and RAS), Franco Angeli ed.

41. Celio Gozi, *Memoria sugli Ebrei a San Marino durante l'ultimo conflitto* (Memorial about the Jews in San Marino during the recent conflict) – Gozi's Collection, RSM.

Russi family had owned a house in San Marino, but it had been sold a few years before the war. When Armando arrived there, he went to live in a house in Contrada Santa Croce, in what was once the Jewish ghetto. The house where he lived had a colorful entrance door, which everybody remembered, made of colored glass, with the upper part shaped in an arch.[42]

His father's cousins, two 60-year-old women, lived with him in the same house as well. Their names were Elisa and Emilia Rossi. In Ancona, they owned a leatherwear store. They were two very active ladies in the Jewish community of the Marche region, especially the youngest one, Emilia, who also collaborated with the regional newspaper of the religious community. She would openly and harshly challenge the proclamation of the Racial Laws there. The two had experienced several problems because of that, which was the reason they were forced to take refuge in San Marino.

They received a warm welcome there. The late Giuseppe Russi was remembered as a highly esteemed person, both among local politicians and the common people.

Giuseppina Tamagnini's mother periodically went to Russi's house to do the cleaning.[43] Actually, they lived only a few meters away from that house. Many people used to go there, especially because, in everybody's opinion, Russi was very kind and hospitable.

Yet, towards the end of 1942, something changed. San Marino had to somehow prove to Adolf Hitler that he could find good xenophobes who hunted the Jews even here. So, they quickly passed a law that forbade intermarriage with people belonging to the Jewish race. The law was sent to Berlin to show the Führer that the people of San Marino were good supporters of the Nazis.

Suddenly, the number of Jews increased. But why?

42. From the interview with Giordano Reffi, RSM.

43. From the interview with Giuseppina Tamagnini, RSM.

CHAPTER 3

THE BOMBING OF MILAN

It was almost sunset, the air was mild, and the sky was clear on October 24, 1942. The traffic was quite intense along the streets of Milan when, at 5:57 pm, the air-raid sirens went off. Not even three minutes had gone by when 73 British Lancaster aircrafts appeared in the sky, at over 6,000 meters in altitude. "*Too soon*", someone exclaimed. Something in the air-raid protection had not worked. Many people were trapped in the streets, or they did not have the time to run into the cellars of the buildings, which were used as shelters at that time. Twelve bombs weighing 4,400 pounds, 2,000 large-caliber incendiary bombs, and more than 28,000 smaller bombs fell on the city. A second raid arrived almost immediately afterwards, but it was disturbed by the thick blanket of smoke caused by the hundreds of fires in progress.

Before the sun went down completely, 135 dead and 331 wounded could already be counted along the streets of the city, and this was just the beginning. At 10:44 pm, the sirens sounded again.[44] At dawn, the roads leading out of town were crowded with refugees fleeing to the countryside by any means possible. Most of them were on foot.

---

44. Achille Rastelli, *Bombe sulla città. Gli attacchi aerei alleati: le vittime civili a Milano* (Bombs on the city. Air-raids by the Allies: civilian victims in Milan); Milano, Mursia 2000.

Otto Ruhl and his wife Rosa were traveling in a small car. They had gone to Milan three or four years before. They were originally from Vienna. Before then, they had tried to escape through France, but the attempt had failed. Otto Ruhl worked for a stationery supply company called Kartro, which had branches all over the world. One of its offices was in Milan, on Via Andrea Doria.[45] Mr. Ruhl was not a mere employee. It seems that he was one of the main partners, but so as not to have any problems, seeing that he was a Jew, he had settled in Milan where he had been working as an employee of the Brazilian branch, from which he received some money periodically. Still today, in São Paulo there is a branch of Kartro, founded in 1939.

Kartro was a leading company in the production of carbon paper, and this turned out to be really useful for the couple. In those years, Otto Ruhl had traveled far and wide throughout the Lombardy region. He was always polite and nice. Everyone liked him. As he was a careful observer, he could understand at a glance whether a person was dangerous or harmless to him. When he walked into an office to sell his carbon paper, he always had a miniature bottle of perfume for the secretary and some excellent contraband tobacco for the boss. Those were the most popular items at the time, and thanks to this method, he was able to make several good friends. The most influential was the Fascist Federal Secretary of Como. Otto Ruhl was just going to see him that morning. He had asked for his help in crossing the Swiss border, but the Federal Secretary had no power to do that. Smugglers, who usually helped the Jews cross the border, stayed away from him, and so did the Swiss border authorities, who did not look kindly upon him. The Federal Secretary suggested he go to San Marino. He had met Giuliano Gozi in the past, so he wrote a letter of recommendation to be handed to him personally. This was exactly what Otto Ruhl did.[46]

---

45. From Otto and Rosa Ruhl's letter, December 20, 1946 – Gozi's collection, RSM.

46. Celio Gozi, *Memoria sugli Ebrei a San Marino durante l'ultimo conflitto* (Memorial about the Jews in San Marino during the recent conflict) – Gozi's Collection, RSM.

A lot of people in San Marino still remember Otto. He was between 50 and 60 years old, a discreet person and always kind to everyone. He was put up in the house owned by the nurse, Vio Cornacchia, of the local hospital. The house was located a very short distance from Giuliano Gozi's house, on Via Giovan Battista Belluzzi 45. We cannot exclude that Gozi himself had found that accommodation for the couple. It should be remembered that Malvina Kohn, "old Mrs. Hendl", had been living in that same house for a long time.

Following the bombing of Milan, other people arrived in San Marino. Regina Grymberg lived in Milan on Via Cesare Mangili 2. Her husband was Carlo Brambilla, a former officer, who had left the Royal Army after he got married and had devoted himself to the import-export of fabrics. In those days, he was held prisoner by the British in India. He had been arrested during a business trip and imprisoned because he was a citizen of an enemy country.

One aspect linked Mrs. Brambilla to San Marino. Regina's maternal aunt had been a famous soprano between the 19th and the 20th centuries. They had the same first name, but her last name was Pinkert. She was born in Warsaw in 1869 and was the wife of Edoardo Morotti, the Honorary Consul of San Marino in Milan. She died in 1931, and the house on Via Mangili, where her niece went to live, was also the Consulate headquarters.[47]

Regina Grymberg was born in Warsaw on December 24, 1907. She lived there up to the end of her university studies, then she moved to Italy with her aunt. Since a very young age, Regina had proven to be very emancipated and not at all submissive to the supremacy of men, as was typical at that time. She loved driving, even recklessly, around the streets of Milan in her uncle's luxurious car.[48] She met Carlo Brambilla there. She also brought her mother, Anna Pinkert, to Milan. Anna was born on October 13, 1874, while her father Gregorio had died several years before. Regina and Carlo had a son, Edoardo, born on March 30, 1939.

47. CDEC Milan, "Personal vicissitude" section, Regina Grymberg Brambilla.

48. Recollection by Edoardo Brambilla Grymberg, Modena.

Well, being Jewish, having her husband captive in India, a mother who spoke only Polish and Yiddish, and a three-year-old child was not enough for Mrs. Brambilla. She also had to cope with the Allied bombings. So, Regina, along with her son and her mother, moved to San Marino in the fall of 1942.

This family's situation led to another amazing discovery, namely that, in the full awareness that they were fleeing Jews, they had been given legal residence permits.

These permits were numbered 245 and 246, issued in 1942 and renewed several times up to the end of 1945 by the Political Inspectorate, which depended on the Secretary of State for Foreign Affairs. Those permits were signed by Inspector Pietro Animali, a well-known policeman in the Fascist period.

The information on those papers was all authentic and they stated one thing very clearly: in San Marino, although racial laws and

Podpis własnoręczny

Warszawa, dn. 14 października 192[illegible] r.

UNIWERSYTET WARSZAWSKI

WYKAZ
WYKŁADÓW I ĆWICZEŃ

Liczba alb. 28439

Stud. Wydz. Humanistycznego
Grynberg Regina
rodem z Warszawy
Immatrykulowana dn. 14 paźd. 1928 r.

Regina Grymberg's university card.
(Centro Documentazione Ebraica Contemporanea, Milano.)
— Courtesy of Edoardo Brambilla Grymberg. —

Regina Grymberg with her uncle Edoardo Morotti, Consul of San Marino in Milan.
— Courtesy of Edoardo Brambilla Grymberg. —

regulations were enacted, they were never applied! In addition, the Italian laws, which the Italian government wanted to be applied also in San Marino, established that non-resident foreign Jews were not to be surveyed, but arrested instead and guarded in certain confinement areas, or expelled, as occurred in Merano.[49]

According to Edoardo Brambilla, or rather, on the basis of what he was told by his mother, because he had no memory of that time as he was too young, they arrived in San Marino after the bombing of Milan, or better after October 22, 1942. His mother had actually asked for a duplicate of her identity card in Milan on December 12 of that year, but something strange came up. Some documents were found testifying that Mrs. Grymberg had sent a trunk of clothing weighing 140 pounds to San Marino on June 26, 1942. There's nothing to object to this. She had probably already prepared herself for the step the bombing eventually forced her to take. The "Renzi" forwarding company sent the trunk to Giovanni Fabiani on behalf of the Brambilla family.

---

49. Gregorio Caravita, *Ebrei in Romagna (1938-1945) dalle leggi razziali allo sterminio* (Jews in the Romagna region (1938-1945) from Racial Laws to extermination), Longo ed., Ravenna.

REPUBBLICA DI SAN MARINO
SEGRETERIA DI STATO PER GLI AFFARI ESTERI
ISPETTORATO POLITICO

PERMESSO DI SOGGIORNO

N. 245 breve 1942

San Marino, li 1°/7/1944

L'ISPETTORE POLITICO

N. B. — I figli minorenni entro tre mesi dal raggiungimento della maggiore età, debbono chiedere ed ottenere permesso di soggiorno a loro intestato.

Cognome GRINBERG
Nome Regina
Padre fu Gregorio
Madre Pinkert Anna
Nato il 24/XII/1907
a Varsavia
Stato Civile in Branbilla
Nazionalità Italiana
Professione Agiata
Residenza Città presso Amati Raffaele

Il presente permesso vale anche per la Moglie
e i figli minorenni Brambilla Edoardo di anni 5

REPUBBLICA DI SAN MARINO
SEGRETERIA DI STATO PER GLI AFFARI ESTERI
ISPETTORATO POLITICO

PERMESSO DI SOGGIORNO

N. 246 breve 1944

San Marino, li 1°/7/1944

L'ISPETTORE POLITICO

N. B. — I figli minorenni entro tre mesi dal raggiungimento della maggiore età, debbono chiedere ed ottenere permesso di soggiorno a loro intestato.

Valevole fino al 30/9/1944

Anna Pinkert and Regina Grymberg Brambilla's residence permits.

(Centro Documentazione Ebraica Contemporanea, Milano)
— Courtesy of Edoardo Brambilla Grymberg. —

Ercole Gardini is convinced that the family lived right in Fabiani's home for a while. He saw that woman many times in the house next to his and so did another neighbor, Carla Nicolini. But along with the receipt of the trunk there were also some receipts of payment for the rent of Raffaele Amati's apartment. Did they really live at Fabiani's house during that first period? According to Edoardo Brambilla, they did not! However, the two families must have been good friends, since it is proven that Fabiani was the one to receive the trunk shipped by the woman. Moreover, she was often seen near their home, which was rather far from where they actually lived.

Another important point to take into consideration is that Raffaele Amati, a well-known local cabinetmaker and carpenter, had joined the Clandestine Communist Party and was the son of Domenico and Anna Amati Rava, a woman from Faenza and also a Jew! This detail helps us to better understand Amati's hospitality towards Grymberg. Definitely, it was not only for economic reasons.

Raffaele Amati and his mother, Anna Rava.
— Courtesy of Fabio Pedini Amati. —

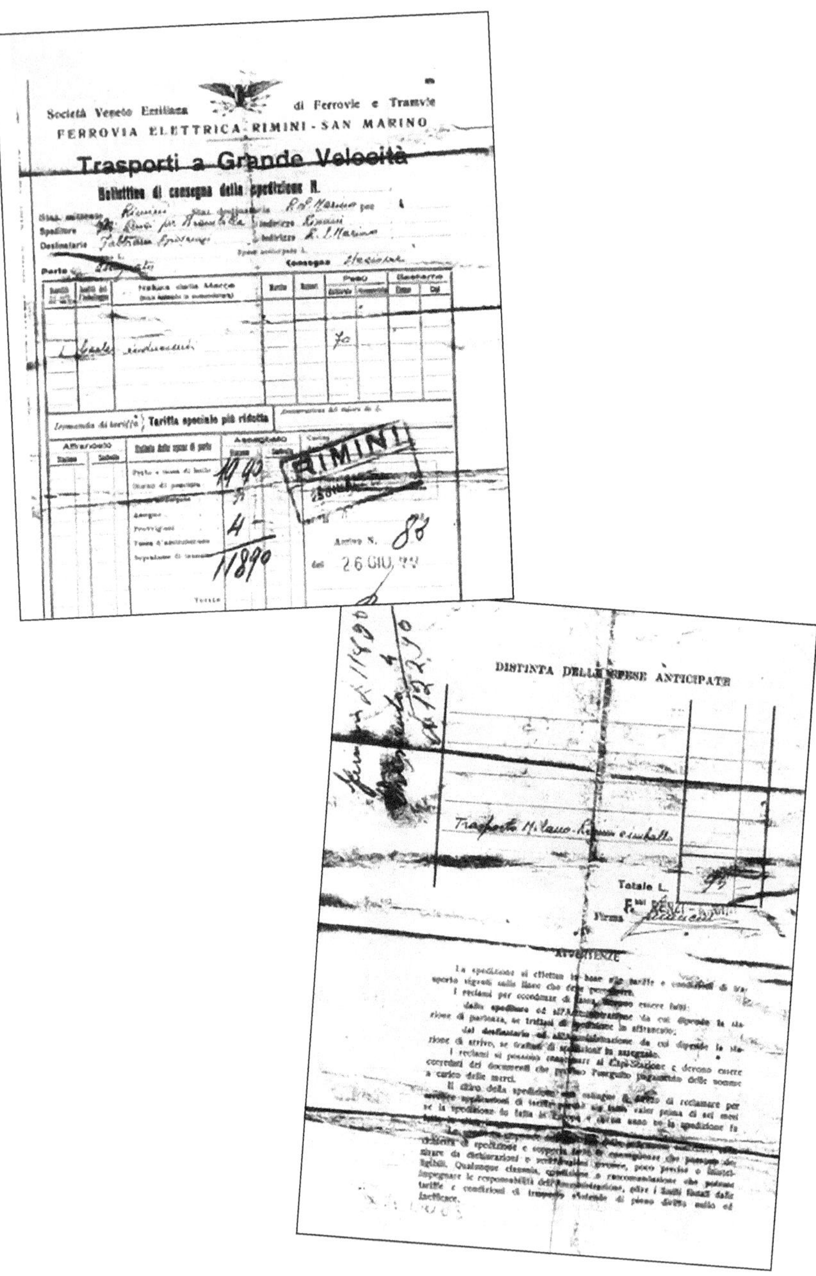

Società Veneto Emiliana di Ferrovie e Tramvie
FERROVIA ELETTRICA RIMINI - SAN MARINO

Trasporti a Grande Velocità

Bollettino di consegna della spedizione N.

Tariffa speciale più ridotta

RIMINI

Arrivo N. 83

del 26 GIU.

DISTINTA DELLE SPESE ANTICIPATE

Trasporto Milano-Rimini cimbalo

Totale L.

Firma

AVVERTENZE

Front and back of a receipt dated June 26, 1942,
for the delivery of Regina Brambilla Grymberg's trunk.
— Courtesy of Edoardo Brambilla Grymberg. —

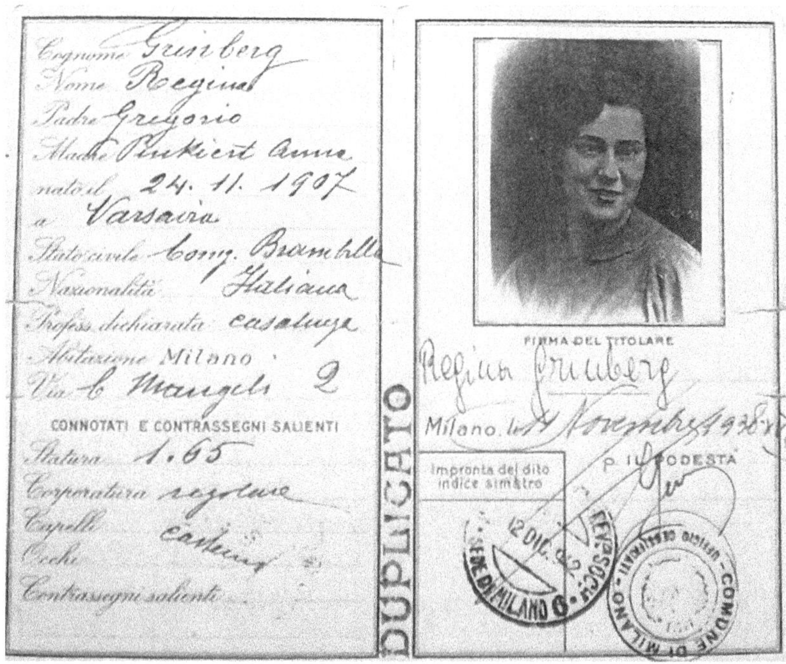

Cognome Grinberg
Nome Regina
Padre Gregorio
Madre [illegible] Anna
nato il 24. 11. 1907
a Varsavia
Stato civile Coniug. Brambilla
Nazionalità Italiana
Profess. dichiarata casalinga
Abitazione Milano
Via C. Mangili 2
CONNOTATI E CONTRASSEGNI SALIENTI
Statura 1.65
Corporatura regolare
Capelli castani
Occhi
Contrassegni salienti

DUPLICATO

FIRMA DEL TITOLARE
Regina Grinberg
Milano, li [illegible] Novembre 1938
P. IL PODESTÀ
Impronta del dito indice sinistro
12 DIC. 42
SEDE DI MILANO
COMUNE DI MILANO

Regina Grymberg's fake identity card with a seal dated December 12, 1942.
— Courtesy of Edoardo Brambilla Grymberg. —

The people of San Marino remembered her as "*la Brambilla.*" Even Celio Gozi remembered her, but only mentioned her, not her mother, and "her little girl". That's right, "a little girl".[50]

According to most people who noticed her, Regina Grymberg Brambilla had a daughter, but obviously, even this little secret could not be hidden from Giuseppina Tamagnini. "*No,*" she said in a whisper, "*it was a boy named Edoardo. His mom always kept his hair long, often in braids. She used to tell him that she had promised his father not to cut his hair until he came back from the war.*"[51] Three photographs of Edoardo, taken back in the 1940s, are still available. In the first one, his hair was long and straight, while in the other two, he had two long braids.

---

50. Celio Gozi, *Memoria sugli Ebrei a San Marino durante l'ultimo conflitto* (Memorial about the Jews in San Marino during the recent conflict) – Gozi's Collection, RSM.

51. From the interview with Giuseppina Tamagnini, RSM.

S.Marino I4 Settembre I943

Riceve dalla Sig Brambilla l'importo 800 (ottocento) del fitto sino al 2 Ottobre I943

In fede

Amati Raffaele

S.Marino li 22 Giugno I945

Sig Regina Brambilla

Ricevo lire (quattromilaottocento) per canone d'affitto per i mesi ,Dicembre,Gennaio,Febbraio Marzo, Aprile,Maggio,I945. lire 4800

In Fede

Amati Raffaele

S.Marino li 2 Maggio I945

Sig Regina Brambilla

Ricevo lire Duemilaquattrocento (£2400) per canone d'affitto per i mesi di Settembre, Ottobre,Novembre. I944

In fede

Amati Raffaele

Receipts issued by Raffaele Amati for the payment of the apartment rented by Regina Grymberg.
— Courtesy of Edoardo Brambilla Grymberg. —

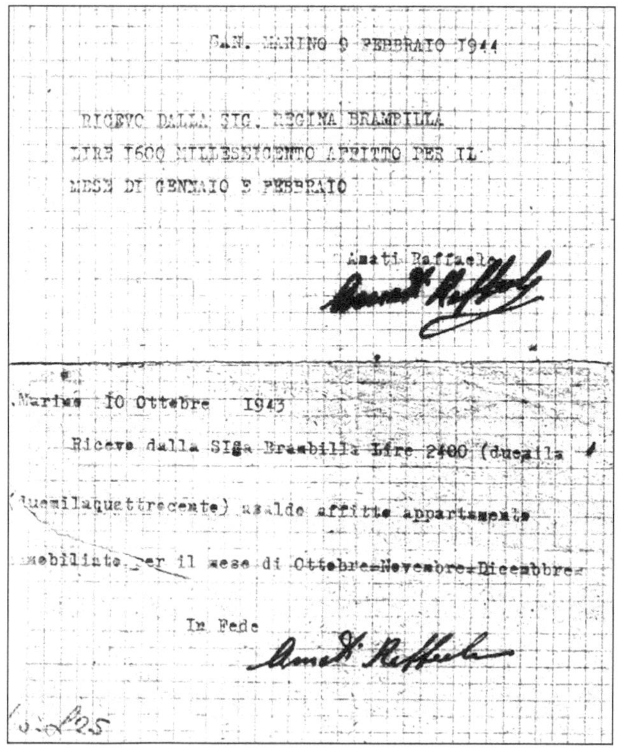

S. MARINO 9 FEBBRAIO 1944

RICEVO DALLA SIG. REGINA BRAMBILLA
LIRE 1600 MILLESEICENTO AFFITTO PER IL
MESE DI GENNAIO E FEBBRAIO

Amati Raffaele

S. Marino 10 Ottobre 1943

Ricevo dalla SIGa Brambilla Lire 2400 (duemila
quattrocento) a saldo affitto appartamento
mobiliato per il mese di Ottobre-Novembre-Dicembre

In Fede

Receipt issued by Raffaele Amati for the payment of the apartment rented by Regina Grymberg.
— Courtesy of Edoardo Brambilla Grymberg. —

When I contacted him for the first time at his house in the province of Modena, he was surprised: "*I'd forgotten the story of the promise, but now I remember. It's true,*" he said emotionally. It already sounded strange to him that someone in San Marino could still remember him, but being aware that someone knew about those details seemed literally incredible to him. "*I remember the walks I would take with my grandmother to the towers and the stones I threw from up there. I thought they would reach the sea. She made me eat tripe every single day.*" Giuseppina Tamagnini remembered when his grandmother took Edoardo to Mr. Albertini's grocery store near his home: "*Edoardo was always scolding that poor old woman because she did not speak a word of Italian. That woman had a heart of gold*".

Regina Grymberg Brambilla with her son Edoardo and her mother Anna Pinkert.
(Centro Documentazione Ebraica Contemporanea, Milano.)
— Courtesy of Edoardo Brambilla Grymberg. —

Several greeting cards from Regina Brambilla have also turned up. She sent them at Christmas and Easter to almost every politician of that period. They were small cards with her name printed on them where she would add a few words of greeting. She was always very polite and elegant. Carla Nicolini also remembers her very well: "*That woman surprised me. She was my mother's age. But while my mother was always dressed in black and wore a handkerchief on her head, Mrs. Brambilla wore young-looking clothes, and her hair was always neatly combed. It was unusual to see a woman of her age dressed so well*".

She lived in the apartment in front of Raffaele Amati's carpenter shop, and rumors were going around of an alleged affair she had with her neighbor, Professor Francesco Balsimelli, a teacher at the local high school at that time. However, it must be said that in those days it was very easy for the people of a small town to say such things. It was enough to see a man and a woman speaking on the street and immediately gossip went around about the affair in progress. Moreover, Francesco Balsimelli was known to be quite sensitive to feminine charm, and Regina Grymberg Brambilla, everybody admitted, had all the charm in the world.

Edoardo Brambilla and his mother, Regina Grymberg Brambilla, in San Marino near the First Tower. (Centro Documentazione Ebraica Contemporanea, Milano.) – Courtesy of Edoardo Brambilla Grymberg. –

In 1942, several people from Bologna also arrived. Among them was an elderly couple from Vienna named Leopold Grünfeld and Bettina Zaitschek. Leopold was born in Vienna on November 9, 1875, and Bettina was originally from Brno in Czechoslovakia, where she was born on December 19, 1879. The couple owned a historic Art Nouveau building in Vienna on the Small Ring, in the heart of the city. The "Kristall Café," a luxurious club with 1,000 seats, was located on the ground floor of that building. Leopold had managed the café for many years after a distinguished military career in the Imperial Army.

From the marriage, which took place in 1902, three children were born: Carl, Edith, and Zita. Unfortunately, the son committed suicide following a love story gone wrong, while the daughters married two Italians, both from Bologna. Edith married Giuseppe Mandelli, while Zita became Mario Guizzardi's wife.

When they arrived in San Marino, the Mandellis already had three children. The youngest was a boy named Ruggero, then there was Vittoria, and the firstborn was Maria José, whom everyone called Baby. But why was she known as Baby by all the people in San Marino? The history and vicissitudes of her family started precisely with that nickname. "*My parents met in Riccione. My mother was there on vacation with her mother and sister,*" recalled Maria José. "*They were staying at the Grand Hotel in Riccione. My father had a house in Cattolica, but in the evening he always went over to the Grand Hotel because he was seeing a girl who was staying there as well. Someone asked my mother to play something on the piano in the lobby. She was a talented pianist. She played a couple of classic songs and then went on with some jazz. At one point, she sang... I cannot give you anything but love, babyyy... My father couldn't believe his ears. He got rid of his girlfriend in a flash and began courting my grandmother, not my mother. He wanted to immediately get on my grandmother's good side. He had no shame. He was very nice and handsome, but also very shameless. He insisted so much that, in the end, my grandmother had to give in. They decided to celebrate the wedding in Vienna. All his relatives and friends arrived from Bologna. It was just like a mass exodus to Austria, but something unexpected happened there. The day after the wedding, my grandfather on my father's side died, so the long march back to Bologna was no longer a wedding procession, but rather a funeral procession. Then, I was born on December 2, 1929. I was the first child, and my parents used to call me Baby, in memory of that song at the Grand Hotel in Riccione, get it? Then Vittoria and Ruggero were born."*[52]

But were Leopold and Bettina really Jews? *"Of course they were! They were non-practicing Jews, but Jews all the same!"* And what prompted everyone to go to San Marino? *"I remember it started when we were on vacation in Cortina. It was 1938... or maybe 1939... I don't remember. Actually, no, it was 1938 because my brother Ruggero was one, so it was 1938. Anyway, we were there when we learned that Hitler had invaded Poland. My mother and my aunt Zita began to cry incessantly and kept saying they wanted our grandparents to get out of Austria. In Bologna, during the days that followed, a woman who was teaching my aunt how to crochet asked her why she was so sad. She confided her concerns and the desire to get her parents to Italy. Is that all? — replied the woman — that's not a problem! My aunt did not know that she was married to a big-shot Fascist who managed to get her two passes for her parents. So, my father, my uncle Mario, and my aunt Zita drove to the Austrian border while my grandparents went there by taxi. Unfortunately, the Italian officials at the border did not let them through. They could only see and talk to each other, remaining on the boundary line, of course. Then, they all agreed to move to another border and try there, but they were stopped there as well, and the same occurred at the next one too. At the end of the day, however, when all hope seemed to be lost... you know, incredible things happen by chance in a lifetime. My uncle gave the documents to an official who exclaimed, "Guizzardi from Sant'Agata Bolognese... are you related to the Mother Superior of the Convent... etc., etc.?"*

"Yes!" replied my uncle, "she's my sister!"

So, it was thanks to Uncle Mario's sister that my grandparents were able to enter Italy."

52. From the interview with Maria José Mandelli, Reggio Calabria.

Maria José Mandelli, nicknamed "Baby," at the age of 13.
— Courtesy of Maria José Mandelli. —

And did you all come to San Marino?

"No, we came to San Marino in 1942. We lived in Bologna for a few years. Then, out of fear of both war and hunger — there was nothing to eat in Bologna — we all fled to Porretta. But we were freezing to death there, so we did not stay long. That is when we came to San Marino. My father bought the house owned by Manlio Gozi, the secretary of the Fascist Party of San Marino, while my uncle got a nice house a little further down the hill. My grandparents were hiding on Mount Carpegna."

But no. Dozens of people claimed they had known your grandparents and asserted that they had lived the entire time in Riziero Para's house, near the train station!

Giuseppe Mandelli and Edith Grünfeld on the day of their wedding in Vienna.
— Courtesy of Maria José Mandelli. —

Giuseppe Mandelli and Edith Grünfeld in a photo taken during the 1950s in Bologna.
— Courtesy of Maria José Mandelli. —

"Really?" She answered, *"My aunt Zita lived close to the station."*

"And her grandparents Leopold and Bettina lived 20 meters away!"

"Really?... However, they hid them from us children. They wouldn't let us meet them. I saw my grandfather Leopoldo again only after the bombing of June 26, 1944. We all ran into the tunnel near the station, and I found him in there. He was in his bathrobe and slippers. He was having a shower when the bombing started... that's why!'

Maria José Mandelli continued with her story about their arrival in San Marino: "As soon as we got there, my father went crazy, literally crazy. We had been dying of hunger up to then... while we could find everything our hearts desired there... He began with roast pork, then roast beef, then pasta... This was heaven for him. It was so good that my father went to get all our relatives one by one and brought them there. In the end, there were 22 of us in that house and my younger sister was not even born yet. By the way, I spoke to her on the phone, and I told her you were coming to interview me. She asked me to remind you to write down that she was born in San Marino. You know, she's very proud of it. Her name is Patrizia Marina."

Gian Piero Gozi underlined: *"My father was in great need of money at that time, so he sold the house to Mandelli for 300,000 liras. It was a bad deal. He could have sold it for three million immediately after the war. We moved into a rented apartment in a building, 50 meters away on the same street."*

It is a fact that everyone in San Marino remembered those families. As soon as he heard the name Mandelli, Giordano Reffi looked up to the sky and exclaimed: "Ah, what a beautiful girl that Baby was." Then, after recovering from that elation, he continued: "Her grandfather was a man of the past. He was so kind and courteous. He behaved in a way that made you feel like you were standing in front of Emperor Franz Joseph. I used to meet him in the evening when there was a party going on. He and his wife often went to them. "Giuseppina Tamagnini explained, "Mandelli and Simone Michelotti set up a cake factory in San Marino."

"La Serenissima," a factory producing traditional local cakes, was founded in San Marino in 1942. But what kind of traditional cakes? We can now try to draw a logical conclusion about what links San Marino to wafers. In fact, San Marino's traditional cake, the so-called "Tre Monti", is nothing more than a wafer: large, round, and covered in delicious chocolate, but always a wafer! We can now assume that when the factory was established, there was a clear Viennese influence on it.

Giovanni Michelotti, one of Simone's sons, said: *"Giuseppe Mandelli had nothing to do with production. He dealt with the marketing of the product. He was the sole distributor... and what a distributor!... What an extraordinary person!"*[53]

Giuseppe Mandelli and Simone Michelotti became friends from the moment they first met. Together, they decided to establish the company: one would handle production while the other worked diligently to market the products throughout central Italy. They were so close that they often alternated their children's roles within the company. Maria José Mandelli recalled frequently visiting the production plant to assist Michelotti in wrapping the cakes, while Giovanni Michelotti accompanied Mandelli to sell them.

The Grünfelds' other daughter, Zita, bought Marino Bollini's house near the station. Everyone remembered her and her husband Mario Guizzardi, a former agent in the "Razzo" company, which produced chemicals for cleaning. They had no children. They were a distinguished couple and participated in the social life of the country. They integrated immediately in a wonderful way.

The two met thanks to Mandelli, who was a very good friend of Guizzardi. Mandelli introduced his sister-in-law to his friend, who eventually became her husband. Even today, the one particular thing that everyone remembers about this couple is that they founded a paint factory called "Colorificio Sammarinese" almost immediately after they arrived in San Marino. When it was established, Giuseppe

53. Statement by Giovanni Michelotti, RSM.

Simone Michelotti at his cake factory "La Serenissima."
— Courtesy of Michelotti's family. —

Mandelli held a small share in the company, while Riziero Para, the owner of the house where Leopold and Bettina were living, held another small percentage.

Towards the end of 1942, other refugees quietly arrived in San Marino. They were much more discreet than the previous ones. Actually, the people there hardly knew anything about them.

The first was a young man from Bologna. Giorgio Zani said he had met a Jew in that period: "*We often met up with the other guys and he was always hanging around here.*"

But how did you know he was Jewish? He answered, "*This was my guess. You know, during the war he had one name, while after the war he suddenly changed it. At that point, I realized that he had to be a Jew. But now I can't remember either his real name or the fake one.*" Maria José Mandelli solved the mystery in a flash: "*His name was Gian Carlo Bonfiglioli. He had changed his name to Bonfigli. You know, Bonfiglioli is a typical Jewish name, while the other one isn't. He lived at the boarding school. The monks put him up, and he often hung out with us. I remember that he had just graduated in engineering.*"

The Colorificio Sammarinese in the 1940s.

Adelia Cesari, Father Cesari's niece, added two more details: "*Mrs. Bonfiglioli's son was my first boyfriend.*" This statement proved that Giancarlo was in San Marino with his mother, yet there was no trace of a Mrs. Bonfiglioli. "*He was taller than me, but when I pointed this out, he always replied 'Parva sed apta mihi,' (you're small but big enough for me).*"[54]

Another important confirmation then emerged. Celio Gozi wrote that he believed some Jews were being housed by the local Franciscan Friars, but no record of this remains. Nothing was documented by the man who, as described by everyone, resembles more a mythological being than a human. Reverend Father Alfredo Cesari, better known as Father Cesari, was born on September 19, 1893.

He had two brothers, Augusto and Dante. They were sons of Cesare Cesari, called "Cisaren de Sartor" (Cesare, the tailor's son). Originally, this family lived in the old town center of San Marino, but at the beginning of the 20th century, Cesare and his brother emigrated to La Spezia, where he made a fortune by winning a contract

54. From the interview with Adelia Cesari, Rimini.

to manufacture and supply all the uniforms for the officers of the Italian Royal Navy. They returned to San Marino in the late 1920s and spent the money they had earned on the purchase of several farmlands in the areas of Fiorina, Domagnano, and Serravalle, as well as others outside San Marino. The Cesaris devoted themselves to agriculture, while Alfredo became a monk. At a young age, he became Father Provincial of the Friars Minor Conventual in Osimo. He was later transferred to Modena, where he became the Rector of the Collegio San Carlo. Finally, in the mid-1930s, Father Cesari returned to San Marino.

Father Alfredo Cesari.
— Courtesy of Adelia Cesari, Rimini. —

The façade of the Convent of Saint Francis in an old photo.
— Courtesy of the State Library, RSM. —

The locals only remembered him by his last name. No one seemed to have ever known his first name. Yet, he was a charismatic figure of that period. He was entrusted with the direction of the Belluzzi boarding school during one of its most challenging times. Everybody said he was a firm man. Alberto Marvelli, a young man originally from Ferrara but adopted by Rimini, brought him a considerable number of refugees from the coast. However, they were not housed in the convent like Bonfiglioli, but rather in the boarding school. This fact highlights this unusual man's protective spirit: Father Cesari was a Franciscan friar, yet he placed the Catholics elsewhere while he kept the Jewish boy under the same roof as him.

CHAPTER 4

1943

Despite the lingering fear in the air, time passed peacefully in San Marino. Following the advice of the Fascist leaders and exercising caution when necessary was enough for people to lead a life that could be described as serene.

The Prefects had relocated small groups of guarded Jews to the towns bordering the Republic of San Marino.

Thanks to the detailed research carried out by Gregorio Caravita, we can now read the chronicles of that confined population. They could not go out before dawn, nor could they stay out after dark, and they could neither send nor receive letters without having them censored: they suffered these and many other limitations that made the lives of those poor wretches a daily ordeal.

In San Marino, instead, it was the party era. In addition to a location at the end of Contrada del Pianello where dancing occurred every night and the restaurant "La Taverna," where this happened occasionally, there was a charming cottage a little further down the hill. It belonged to the Malagola family, who were supposedly in Hungary, where Mr. Malagola had another residence. Some people had doubts about this and assumed that he was more likely to be in England, where the daughters from his first marriage had lived for many years. However, his daughter confirmed that they lived in Budapest at the time. Well, Malagola had rented that beautiful house to a family from Forlì. They owned a well-known sausage factory, and their name was Neri. Mr. Neri and his wife, Renata, stocked an impressive assortment of liquors of all brands in the house basement.

"There must have been between 300 and 500 bottles."— pointed out the very nice man, Giordano Reffi, — *"There was a party every evening. We drank every single bottle, starting from the best ones. At the end, only some Cognac Public was left. It tasted like rubbing alcohol... but we drank that as well!"*[55]

The elderly Grünfeld couple, along with their daughter Zita and son-in-law Mario Guizzardi, were often present at those parties. They were always friendly and polite to everyone. They would never miss any of those social events, where they consistently behaved in a regal and exemplary manner, unlike the young people of San Marino. *"The combination of snow and liquor made us take a step forward and three backward when we left that house,"* said Reffi.

Did all this continue until the arrival of the front? *"No, it lasted until the liquor ran out, then we found another place."*

It snowed heavily during the winter of 1943. *"One morning,"* said Maria José Mandelli, *"the snow was so high that we had to climb out of the window to get out of the house."* Yet, the cold weather was offset by genuine human warmth. On those occasions, did any of them tell you they were Jewish? *"Of course, Zita told me!... And the two old people as well,"* replied Reffi. But were there any racist attitudes towards them? *"No, we never had that kind of polemic here!"*[56]

This use of the term "polemic" is quite interesting. The government in Italy created six different state agencies that, under the orders of the Ministry of the Interior and carried out by public security units, ensured strict compliance with an ever-expanding list of racial laws, which grew longer each day. In addition, propaganda promoted the unanimous condemnation of those belonging to the Jewish race. Well, in San Marino, all of this was summed up in the word "polemic."

And while almost everybody in their houses was waiting for the three usual sounds announcing the bulletin of Radio London to

55. From the interview with Giordano Reffi, RSM.

56. From the interview with Giordano Reffi, RSM.

hear the news that counterbalanced the propaganda of the Italian regime, life went on peacefully... or nearly so. Not a day passed without squads of Blackshirts roaming around and making trouble: once they broke the windows of Albertini's shop, then they destroyed Rufo Reffi's glassware or they punched Ermenegildo Gasperoni, a veteran of the Spanish War, in the face. For that reason, they considered him their punching ball. With the blessing of the Fascist Party, those bullies roamed the streets of the country, reminding everyone who held the power.

During the spring of 1943, a large family from Modena came to San Marino. They rented two adjoining apartments in an area called "the Crucifix." The apartments were owned by two different people: one was Giovanni Fabiani, the man who had helped Regina Grymberg move her belongings from Milan to San Marino; the other was Giuseppe Gardini. It seems that these two men were the only ones who saw the entire family: Salvatore Donati, his wife Graziella Schiller, and their children Amedeo, Raffaele, Andrea, Anna, and Maurizio.[57]

The local people could only remember the father and the eldest son, Amedeo. Some claimed that Amadeo would sometimes go chasing birds with a slingshot in the woods under the Third Tower with the other children of San Marino.

Salvatore Donati, a chemist, was the son of Mandolino Donati and Irma Ravenna. He belonged to an ancient family originally from Finale Emilia who had moved to Modena in the second half of the 16th century after they had been given permission to introduce buckwheat into the territory controlled by the noble Este family. That grain would save that place, affected by the plague described by Manzoni, from starvation. At a young age, Donati took over his father's company and soon became a point of reference at the national level in the production and processing of leather.[58]

57. From Amedeo Donati's recollections – kind courtesy. Of CDEC Milan.

58. Article from a newspaper published in Modena without title, guarded at the CDEC in Milan.

Salvatore had an uncle, Angelo Donati, who was an attorney and a former aviator during the First World War. He emigrated to France, where he worked as a banker and served as the Consul of San Marino in Paris from 1925 to 1932. In 1927, Donati went down in history for setting the altitude record with his airplane: 11,827 meters. However, he is still remembered today not for his feats in aviation, but for the help he provided to many French Jews during the years of racial persecution. He was forced to flee from France because he was officially wanted by the SS. Nonetheless, he managed to help 2,500 Jews escape from Nice before leaving. The French army knew him by the derogatory nickname of the "Pope of the Jews."[59]

When he returned to Italy in early 1943, Donati decided to execute the largest escape plan ever implemented since biblical times. Through an agreement reached with the British and American diplomats present at the Vatican, and with the support of DELASEM, the organization for assisting Jews in Genoa, he resolved to help 7,000 French Jews flee to together to Palestine.[60]

Salvatore went to San Marino, surely thanks to his uncle Angelo, who chose not to go there at that time. Celio Gozi recalled an episode about Donati, reported to him by Quinto Reffi, who was officially an undertaker at the Montalbo cemetery but also worked as a waiter at the Hotel Titano. He did not specify the date when this happened, but one day Salvatore Donati was having lunch alone at the hotel restaurant and severely reproached Quinto Reffi for serving him pork, which was forbidden by his religion.

It is unclear whether the following occurred as a result of that incident, but another recollection was associated with the Donatis. This one involved Salvatore's son, Amedeo. It is said that one day in

---

59. Paolo Veneziano, *Angelo Donati, un ebreo modenese tra Italia e Francia* (Angelo Donati, a Jew from Modena between Italy and France), catalogue of the exhibition organized during a conference about Angelo Donati, Modena, January 27, 2004.

60. Liliana Picciotto Fargion, *Il libro della memoria. Gli Ebrei deportati dall'Italia (1943-1945)* (The book of memory. The Jews deported from Italy (1943-1945)), Milano, Mursia, 2002, new updated edition.

San Marino, he ate, with great pleasure, a plate of pasta with meat sauce made with pork. According to local witnesses, this surprised everyone, as they all knew about the Jewish precept by that time.

Soon after the Donatis' arrival, another person came to San Marino, yet for many days, even the most curious busybodies knew nothing of his presence.

Camillo Castiglioni was the son of the Rabbi of Trieste. He was born in 1879. After finishing high school, he worked in Padua as a bank clerk but remained there only for a short time. He then emigrated to Vienna, where he had an impressive career and was nicknamed "Stinnes, the Shark."

He devoted himself to high finance, founding banks and financial institutions. He quickly became one of the major shareholders of Deutsche Bank. He caught the attention not only of the greatest businessmen of the period but also of influential figures, such as Emperor Franz Joseph of Habsburg, who awarded him the Iron Cross. Anyone with an idea to be developed would approach him: inventors, engineers... anyone. He had significant capital at his disposal and the full intention to massively expand his financial empire.

Among the companies founded by Castiglioni that will remain in history, we can mention only a few, since there were over 170 in total. For example, there is "Hansa-Brandenburg," which Castiglioni established by merging some of his factories. Its first business activity was producing blimps, and later airplanes, with designers like Ernst Heinkel and Ferdinand Porsche. Produced in those plants was the famous "Albatros," a thorn on the side of the renowned aviator Francesco Baracca, against whom he fought several times during World War I.

The "Bayerische Motoren Werke" was founded in Munich on July 21, 1917. Its name can be literally translated as "Bavarian Industry of Motors," and today it is known worldwide as "BMW." Camillo Castiglioni owned a third of its shares and was also a business consultant. In 1921, he became Chairman of the General Credit Bank in Vienna and later founded the Castiglioni Banking House. He was also a great patron of the arts: he built a large theater under the direction of Max Reinhardt, a grand museum in the Austrian capital, and he financed the Salzburg Festival.

Yet, all this did not last forever. Castiglioni's empire underwent several jolts. His art collection was confiscated after WWI and auctioned off to repay the state an amount equivalent to $ 4.2 million, lost by the Viennese banks due to his companies. This was the only way to lift the arrest warrant issued against him for fraud.

On Monday, October 6, 1924, Time magazine dedicated a lengthy article to Castiglioni: he was described as the richest man in central Europe, but without scruples. To increase his capital, he had dismantled entire countries and had calmly awaited the announced crash while safely in Italy with his Fascist friends.

However, Camillo Castiglioni was an incredibly resourceful man and soon managed to re-emerge at the highest levels of finance. He did not stop even after the proclamation of Racial Laws, when he had to leave the huge villa he owned on the shore of Lake Grundlsee and flee to Switzerland. In the meantime, Friedrich Wolffhardt decided he would use the building to house the largest library in the world. Obviously, it would be called "Führerbibliothek" and, once completed, it would contain one million volumes.

But as we said, Stinnes could not just hang around doing nothing. During the time he spent in the Swiss Alps, he built a petrochemical group called "IPSA," with the collaboration of Attorney Meyer, the former head of the Lower House of the Swiss Confederation, and Chairman of the Liberal Party. Meyer was more than a mere collaborator: he was Castiglioni's spitting image. Then something went wrong. In early June 1943, the Swiss government received two notes from the OSS, which was the equivalent of the CIA at that time. They declared that Meyer was none other than Castiglioni's figurehead and that the latter did not invest his own money, but rather the treasure that Benito Mussolini and Galeazzo Ciano had stolen from the Italians during the long period of dictatorship.[61]

61. Alessandra Farkas, *Corriere della Sera*, October 8, 1996, pag. 13.

Camillo Castiglioni in a photo dating back to the 1920s.

So, it was on June 16, 1943, that the Swiss government finally expelled Camillo Castiglioni! Many wondered: where did Stinnes go? He was hunted down by the SS because he was a Jew, coveted by the Americans who were eager to know the darkest secrets of European finance guarded in his mind, and who knows how many others wanted him... It is normal to think that, given the charges of being Mussolini's money launderer, he would probably go and ask him for refuge! But he didn't! Guess where he ended up? ...

You can still hear the elders of San Marino telling the story, almost as if it were a joke, about when they ran into "the friar in silk socks" walking along the streets of the town. Everyone laughed at that fake monk, dressed in a habit and sandals, who insisted on wearing those expensive socks. He tried his best to play the part, but none of the people who lived there were fooled by him.

One of the first to realize that Castiglioni was not a monk was Alvaro Casali. His son Aroldo remembered, *"My father was called to the Franciscan convent by Father Cesari. There was someone with a toothache; he immediately saw that he was not a monk."*[62]

So it happened that, as St. Jerome was able to tame the lion by removing a thorn from its paw, Dr. Alvaro Casali became a great friend of Camillo Castiglioni's by healing his toothache. *"He would spend the whole day at my house,"* continued Aroldo Casali, *"He liked chatting with my mother and was really fond of my brother Libero, who was a baby then. I'll always remember him sitting on the couch at home with his chin resting on the silver handle of his walking stick. He would occasionally doze off. He had made many friends in San Marino; he knew how to be unpretentious with common people and sophisticated with intellectuals. Just think. He used to spend half the day chatting with a shopkeeper in Borgo Maggiore, close to our house. His name was Marino Stacchini but everyone called him "Carett" (Cart). He had a tiny little shop where he sold everything, from nightgowns to salted cod."*

In his memorial, Celio Gozi mistakenly called him "Alfio." This might have been the fake name that Castiglioni had chosen for himself. He wrote that he used to play cards with the Italian Consul, Vincenzo Guglielmi, and that he often crossed the border disguised as a monk because "he had to do so to make ends meet." He probably went to Rimini to send and receive letters that allowed him to continue managing his empire. Then, Gozi also quoted Quinto Reffi, the undertaker-waiter of Hotel Titano. He affirmed as well: "I noticed immediately that that man was not a monk."

62. From the interview with Aroldo Casali, RSM.

However, the people of San Marino posed no threat to him. He was very pleased with his new modest homeland as well as with its inhabitants. The important thing was to keep this hidden from the Germans.

It seems incredible that someone like Camillo Castiglioni would devote himself to a cloistered lifestyle. It was the same Castiglioni nicknamed "the shark of finance"; the same man who had bought the car personally owned by the Kaiser so that he would be admired while going to the theater; the same man who had constantly lived in the footlights in a Vienna that looked like a vintage postcard. It seems impossible, yet that is just what happened!

Aroldo Casali said: "*I remember he came to San Marino in mid-1943 and left in 1945. My father took him to Rome in his car. He said he had a villa in the Parioli district.*"

How Castiglioni arrived in San Marino is a mystery. The only connection suggested by instinctive deduction is a ring, which can still be seen today on Maria José Mandelli's finger. The emblem of the Emperor of Austria is in the center of it. She said, "*It was originally a tie clip, then it was turned into a ring. Emperor Franz Joseph of Habsburg gave it to my grandfather Leopold. He also gave him the silver tea service right there,*" she pointed at it. "*That was his wedding gift.*"[63]

So, I read over again the interview I had previously had with Aroldo Casali. He said, "*Camillo Castiglioni was a great friend of the Emperor of Austria. He had a house whose property bordered one of the Emperor's residences. He said he often visited him because they had a small gate in common that gave access to both properties.*"[64]

Did Leopold Grünfeld and Camillo Castiglioni therefore meet in Vienna? They probably did!

Did they meet thanks to the Emperor? Maybe!

Did Leopold Grünfeld help Castiglioni come to San Marino? We might never know this for sure, but at the moment, it is the only connection that can be made.

---

63. From the interview with Maria José Mandelli, Reggio Calabria.

64. From the interview with Aroldo Casali, RSM.

Translation of a portion of the last page of the letter written by Camillo Castiglioni to his friend Alvaro Casali on August 27, 1952. Among the memories contained in the text, Castiglioni admits he was hiding in San Marino: *"I spent a year there, and you seem not to remember that it was actually a matter of life and death every single day. In fact, you might not have known who I really was, but the Germans were quite*

CAMILLO CASTIGLIONI — 2 —

ha fatto tutte le sue proposte per il profondo affetto che continua e continuerà a nutrire per il Vostro Paese. Ho passato lì un anno e tu sembri non ricordare che si è trattato giornalmente e letteralmente di vita o di morte, perchè se Voi non avete mai saputo chi ero veramente, i tedeschi lo sapevano benissimo e questa era la ragione del mio terribile pericolo. Solo con i documenti falsi e con le bugie di Padre Arturo e di Padre Cesari sono arrivato a salvarmi la vita. Sono cose che un uomo dei miei sentimenti e del mio cuore non dimentica quando aveva sessant'anni! Ora forse finirete per capire perchè mi ostino a voler far del bene a San Marino, sapendo che potrei farlo. Il Governo di Israele mi ha scritto due anni fa: " Lei ha fatto delle cose talmente grandi nella Sua vita, che dovrebbe ora coronare la Sua opera, facendo qualche cosa di grande per il nostro paese". Non me la sono sentita, perchè non intraprendo mai un grande lavoro, se non ho la sicurezza di portarlo a buon fine e quella volta erano comunisteggianti e l'America, dopo aver dato per loro - specialmente gli Ebrei americani - decine di milioni di dollari, si era raffreddata moltissimo. Ora il nuovo governo è nettamente democratico e tutto va già meglio.

Giusto questo esempio Vi dimostra cosa sarei in grado di fare per San Marino e ciò naturalmente senza cambiare rumorosamente la Vostra politica. Avete visto che ho fatto la stessa cosa con Tito, al quale non ho domandato sacrifici impossibili, sono bastati alcuni colpi di timone . . .

Rispondi se vuoi e se credi che abbia scopo di farlo.

Ti abbraccio

in immutabile affetto

Dott. Alvaro Casali

San Marino

The last page of Camillo Castiglioni's letter to Alvaro Casali dated August 27, 1952.
— Courtesy of Aroldo Casali, RSM. —

Villa Castiglioni on the shore of Lake Grundlsee.
It had to become the largest library in the world.

aware of it. That was the reason for my terrible danger. Only thanks to Father Arturo and Father Cesari's fake documents and lies was my life spared. These are things that a man of my sentiment and heart will never forget..."

This is the only document ever found in which Castiglioni directly and unequivocally admits to having lived at the Convent protected by the friars. Furthermore, it is one of the rare occasions when Castiglioni signs a letter with his full name; on other occasions, he used to sign with the acronym "CC".

MARCO ARA'S GOLD ANNOUNCES THE FALL OF FASCISM

Yet that idyllic situation could not last forever. A small country like this could not even then live without the influence of Italian politics. More or less on the same days when the Allies landed undisturbed in eastern Sicily, thanks to the complicity of the Italian American mafia, the Fascist leader Giuliano Gozi knocked on the door of Carla Nicolini's house. "*He looked worried. He and my father locked themselves in the study, and then, before leaving, I remember they hugged each other like two people saying their farewells forever. At that moment, I realized I was going to live through a tragic historical moment. I asked immediately, "Dad, what did Giuliano say to you? It seemed like something really bad.*" Then my father told me everything. I was the only one to be told because I was the oldest daughter. He explained that Giuliano Gozi had come to tell him, "*Look Peppino, we're preparing ourselves for some very dramatic times; Fascism is about to fall. I don't want them to find me with all these gold bars. They'll think I got rich just to stay in power." Just think that the Gozis died in poverty instead. I have always been against fascism, but as I love the truth more than my political choices, I must admit that the Gozis were honest people from that point of view. In other words, Giuliano asked my father, should he still be alive after the war, to take those ingots to Marco Ara in Venice. A few days later, the famous Grand Council of Fascism took place. During that meeting, Galeazzo Ciano, along with other early Fascists, planned the coup d'état that overthrew Mussolini... And I assure you that this story is true! I heard everything with my own ears!*"[65]

It is said that the Gozi brothers waited for the news of the fall of fascism at the café in Hotel Titano. Someone was amazed that when Giuliano Gozi heard the news on the radio, he remained motionless. There was not a single crease on his face, which looked as if it had turned to marble.

As Professor Nicolini would say, many years later, he had been waiting for that moment for several days. He had prepared himself for a long time to take the step that history was demanding he carry out.

On July 27, the Captains Regent, Marino Michelotti, and Bartolomeo Manzoni Borghesi, bet everybody to the draw and wrote the manifesto announcing the dissolution of the San Marino Fascist Party. In the meantime, in Alvaro Casali's office in Rimini on Via Cairoli, some anti-Fascists were meeting to agree on what should be done in the days to follow.[66]

On July 28, the insurgents gathered at the theatre in Borgo Maggiore. They held a rally there and then paraded over to the Public Palace. The procession was led by Remy Giacomini, Teodoro Lonfernini, Alvaro Casali, Fausto Amadori, and Ermenegildo Gasperoni. Some of them requested and obtained permission to speak with the Captains Regent, except for Gasperoni, who was left standing outside the door.[67]

During the meeting, which lasted for a couple of hours, they decided to dissolve Parliament and call for new elections on the fol-

---

65. From the interview with Carla Nicolini, RSM.

66. Alvaro Casali, *Rimembranze di un terribile periodo: Fascismo e guerra* (Memories of a terrible period: Fascism and war), Grafiche Sammarinesi Della Balda, 1980, RSM.

67. Gildo Gasperoni – *Itinerario Politico: a San Marino e in Europa in difesa della democrazia* (Political itinerary: in San Marino and Europe in defense of democracy) – A.I.EP. Editrice, 1983, RSM.

lowing September 5th. At the end of the meeting, this decision was announced to the crowd, who had been eagerly awaiting that moment, from the balcony of the Public Palace.

Only one list, called "San Marino Committee for Freedom," was constituted. The impetuous Ermenegildo Gasperoni was once again excluded from this list as well. He had a heated discussion with Teodoro Lonfernini as he reminded the founder of the San Marino Communist Party that Badoglio had announced Italy would continue to fight side by side with Germany and that the arrival of the Allies was still far away, so they were not out of danger yet. At his insistence, Lonfernini added, "*We'll leave a job for you as a street cleaner.*"[68]

A provisional government composed of thirty members was established. It paved the way for free elections, and even some dissenting Fascists were admitted at the last minute. Following the dissolution of the Republican Guard and the Fascist Youth organizations, which occurred on August 4, elections were held on September 5 in a rather tense atmosphere. It was difficult even for the calmest and the most responsible people to control the spirits of those who, for twenty years, had endured the harassment of the dictatorship and were now shouting for revenge.[69]

Someone had considered that something worse might occur. Others, like Teodoro Lonferini, feared it would. In the end, the worst did arrive. While elections were being held in this small country, the Allies, who had already landed in Sicily, began to move their troops from the island to Calabria. On Wednesday, September 8th, it was announced that Marshal Pietro Badoglio had signed an armistice.

This made Hitler furious, and four days later, during a raid, his soldiers freed Mussolini from his prison in Campo Imperatore, on the Gran Sasso mountain. He was physically carried onto a small

---

68. Gildo Gasperoni – *Itinerario Politico: a San Marino e in Europa in difesa della democrazia* (Political itinerary: in San Marino and Europe in defense of democracy) – A.I.EP. Editrice, 1983, RSM.

69. Verter Casali - *Appunti di Storia* (History notes), in *Il Corriere Sammarinese,* Issue no. 45, Friday, May 15, 2004, RSM.

plane nicknamed "Stork" and taken to northern Italy.[70] There, he established the Italian Social Republic, better known as the "Republic of Salò."

San Marino faced a new problem: as soon as it regained its freedom and democracy, it found itself immersed in a stormy sea. The Germans swiftly invaded Italy, whose army had no leadership and was completely helpless. Military violence and abuse of any kind spread throughout.

Drifters, deserters, criminals, and, some said, even spies arrived in this small Republic from everywhere. Among them was a flashy lady who lived at the Hotel Titano for several months. She came from Rimini, where she had been a teacher. She went by the name of Albertina Crico, but her real name was Roxanne Pitt: she was a British spy. *"She always wore large bows in her hair. We children used to call her "the spy" because you could see from afar that she was a spy. But we didn't know whether she was acting for the British or the Germans. Then we realized she was on the British side because when the Germans arrived, she disappeared,"* said Giuseppina Tamagnini.[71]

In 1957, Roxanne Pitt wrote a novel called "The shy spy," published in Italy by Longanesi. The prologue was written by the former head of British Intelligence. In the book, Pitt also recalled the days she spent in San Marino. It must be said, however, that, apart from the fact that she had definitely stayed at the Hotel Titano at the time, all the other statements were purely fiction. For example, it is not true, as she instead wrote, that you could dance every night at the restaurant "La Taverna." Of course, there were some dance parties, as stated by the local inhabitants, but they occurred only occasionally. It is also unlikely that her contact there was a barmaid working at the Titano restaurant, from whom she would receive messages that were then handed over to a fisherman in Rimini. The people of San Marino remembered that she was staying there alone, while she wrote

70. Mimmo Franzinelli, *RSI – La Repubblica del Duce 1943-1945* (RSI – the Duce's Republic 1943-1945), Mondadori, 2007, Milan (pag. 6).

71. Jewish Museum of Merano, kind courtesy of Rosanna Pruccoli.

that she had a little girl and her nurse with her. She also believed San Marino was a "nest of spies ready to sell information both to the Axis and the Allies."

Some people believed this declaration to be true. It must be said, instead, that after carefully checking historical facts and documents of those days, only two spies lived in San Marino at that time, and Pitt was one of them. Moreover, she left San Marino on January 15, 1944 to go to the Puglia region, not to Rome as she wrote in her novel.[72]

Going back to the Jews living in San Marino, in the fall of 1943 the situation got stickier for them. On September 24, General Kappler received a telegram in Rome with the order to start deportations to proceed to the "Final Solution" of the Jews. We do not know exactly how, but this maximum danger warning reached San Marino too. There, too, people feared possible raids by the SS. Officially, the newspaper "Brescia Repubblicana" published the news that all the Jews had been deported to concentration camps only on December 1. Three days later, the Milan newspaper "Il Fascio" went into a little more detail: *to create a civilization where not only native Jews but also those who are Jewish in their spirit and soul cannot live.*[73] The news, however, had leaked before those dates. The Jews in San Marino had different reactions: the two sisters, Emilia and Elisa Rossi, were afraid of being caught, so they left their relative Armando Russi's house in a hurry to take refuge in a hideout in the Marche region, which they defined as "*safer.*"[74]

There were several moments of anxiety. The first serious incident was recorded on October 5, when a commando of the SS entered the territory of San Marino in two armored cars, spreading panic everywhere. They then raided the office of the Captains

72. From the interview with Amedeo Montemaggi, Rimini.

73. Mimmo Franzinelli, quoted work.

74. Celio Gozi, *Memoria sugli Ebrei a San Marino durante l'ultimo conflitto* (Memorial about the Jews in San Marino during the recent conflict) – Gozi's Collection, RSM.

Regent, Marino Della Balda and Sante Lonfernini, with guns in hand, and ordered the two heads of state to hand over five radical citizens. Among them was the "militiaman," that is Ermenegildo Gasperoni, as well as all the British war prisoners who had escaped from detention and found refuge on Mount Titano.

They were searching for two British soldiers who had escaped from a prison camp in Anghiari. It was rumored that a veterinarian from Verucchio had betrayed them and informed the Germans about the runaways' supposed hideout in San Marino. At that point, the Germans captured three anti-Fascists and took them across the border to the village of Montelicciano. There, they entertained themselves by reenacting their prisoners' execution before releasing them.[75]

On October 8, more than a hundred Wehrmacht soldiers crossed the border and seized a large number of cars. They loaded them up with everything they could find and burglarized every home. They even went into Raffaele Amati's carpentry, but when they saw the caskets he had built on display all in a row, they made a gesture to ward off any bad luck and left.[76] It did not even cross their minds to open them up; otherwise, they would have found tons of sausages and cheeses that the clever carpenter had hidden there, fearing hard times. The looting of October 8 was just one of the many robberies and raids carried out during those days, not only by the German troops but also by drifters, deserters, and prisoners on the run. "It was said that among them were also those who had made the attack on the Diana movie theater in Milan," explained Gian Piero Gozi. "My father and his brothers were so scared that when one of them had to leave the house, the others would follow him all in single file. Each one would have his hand in his pocket... holding onto a gun!"[77]

Salvatore Donati fled to the north with his wife and five children. No one in San Marino noticed that they were missing, especial-

75. Antonio Montanari, *I giorni dell'ira* (The days of rage), Il Ponte ed., Rimini.

76. Fabio Pedini Amati's recollection, RSM.

77. From the interview with Gian Piero Gozi, RSM.

ly because, as already remarked, they were one of the most discreet families there. It must have been around October 10: he fled to the Lombardy region, where he knew Angelo Luzzani, a well-known attorney from Como, who arranged for their escape to Switzerland.

The smugglers who were supposed to accompany the family were not ready, so they asked the Donatis to wait for a few days. Then, they all went to Mario Verzolla's home in Monza. He was a friend and customer of Donati's tannery, so he put them up until they fled on the night of October 16, 1943.

On that same day, a house-to-house search began in Rome at 5:30 am: it would end two days later with the deportation of 1,024 Jews at a time on a cattle train heading to Auschwitz.

Returning to the Swiss border, someone mentioned that the smugglers transported the fugitives, the Donatis, through the woods of Mount Bisbino, above Cernobbio. Just across the border, they were intercepted by a patrol that arrested them. They were taken to a collection center and identified there.

Salvatore was not with his family that night. He joined them a few days later. His young children and wife were accompanied by his uncle, Angelo Donati, the former Consul of San Marino in Paris.[78] Even up to the present time, it has always been said that Angelo Donati, before fleeing to Switzerland, had been hiding in Tuscany. He wanted to go back to Nice, but the SS had discovered his plan and were waiting for him in his office. So, he had remained hidden away in the surroundings of Florence. But now it turns out that he crossed the Swiss border with his relatives who had taken refuge in San Marino. Was he on Mount Titano as well? Did he try to organize the mass exodus of thousands of French Jews from San Marino? This question is more than legitimate since he had indicated the small Republic to his nephew as the place to take refuge. Angelo Donati had been Consul of San Marino for many years, and he had met many important figures from that place. Moreover, Salvatore Donati did

78. CDEC Milan – Letter by Amedeo Donati dated March 2, 2001 – "Personal vicissitude" section.

have a large family. Still, it must be remembered that when he arrived on Mount Titano, he rented two apartments, one owned by Fabiani and another by Gardini. Was he waiting for someone else? At the end of August, Angelo Donati had gone to Rome, where he had met General Badoglio. They had agreed to prepare four ships that would leave from the port of Genoa and transport as many Jews as possible. There were rumors that 7,000 of them were ready to leave. The ships were the "*Duilio, Giulio Cesare, Saturnia, and Vulcania*", and DELASEM had offered to pay for the expenses. In those days, Angelo Donati also met with the U.S. Ambassador, Titman, and the British Ambassador, Osborne, at the Vatican. They both knew about the mass transfer that was being organized. Badoglio had been assured that it would take weeks before the news of the armistice signed on September 3 would be disclosed. However, on September 8, Eisenhower surprisingly communicated the fact to the radio, causing the immediate German invasion of Italy and the final halt of "Operation Donati."[79]

Everybody in San Marino heard the news of the possible raids. "*Mrs. Neri from Forlì warned us about them*", said Maria José Mandelli. She was probably referring to that Fernanda Neri living in the Malagola house where all those parties used to take place. "*She said to my father: 'Be careful, Sir. They are also taking away children with mixed blood'. There was a heated discussion. At that time, my mother was pregnant with Patrizia, and she exclaimed: 'If they come here, they have to find me alone, the other children have to save themselves.' So, they decided to hide us.*"[80]

In that house, there were not only mixed-blooded children but also the children of Mandelli's relatives who had arrived later. Eight children were living under the same roof, and they were all in danger

79. *Mémorial de la shoah, FR - Archives - CCXVIII-66_001 - Exposé, non daté, d'Angelo Donati, décrivant les démarches entreprises par les Italiens pour le sauvetage des Juifs dans la zone d'occupation italienne en France.* (Memorial about the Holocaust, FR – Archives - CCXVIII-66_001 – Presentation, undated, in which Angelo Donati describes the steps taken by the Italians to save the Jews in the French areas occupied by Italy).

80. From the interview with Maria José Mandelli, Reggio Calabria.

The house where the Mandelli family lived.
— Photograph by Filippo Pruccoli. —

because they could easily be mistaken for Edith Grünfeld's children. Then, they reached an agreement with a neighbor, a member of the Balsimelli family, nicknamed "Pandemonium." His name was Attilio Balsimelli, and what people remembered of him was the wonderful evenings spent listening to the sound of his violin, accompanied by his daughter Dina. He was willing to hide them all. This occurred only during daylight hours; in the still of the night, every movement would have been noticed well in advance from the top of the hill, thus giving everyone time to find a safe place to hide.

"So, every morning, we all went out early, hand in hand, and crossed the garden. We went to hide in Balsimelli's cellar. In that basement, there was a narrow slit which looked out onto the sidewalks. You could only see the shoes of those passing by. We spent the whole day looking through that slit to see if those who walked by were wearing normal shoes or military boots. We were terrified that they would go and take our mother away" said Maria José Mandelli.[81]

In the meantime, three German officers moved into the house belonging to the little Mandelli children's aunt. But why didn't they

81. Ibid.

go to the Hotel Titano like all the others? *"They liked that house so much that they decided to settle down there. They did not have to ask for anyone's permission, so they stayed there for several days,"* explained Maria José. *"My aunt Zita, spent all day long in the kitchen with her maid cooking for them, and in the evening, they would also play bridge together."* Didn't they notice that she was a Jew? *"No, never. Luckily, no one ever snitched on us."*[82]

On October 13, Giuliano Gozi gave the government his full availability to become San Marino's Special Delegate with the belligerent armies, but his offer was instantly turned down.[83]

On October 23, the Great and General Council resolved to delegate the exercise of powers to a Council of State formed by twenty members. In the session which followed on October 28, the Captains Regent took the floor to say, *"As a result of the painful events that occurred during the first few days of this month of October, events which have disturbed the peace of this town, a local situation has arisen that has urged the political bodies and as well as other groups of citizens to come to a peaceful truce in order to cope with this sad situation all together. Meetings were held between the various members of the Council, and between them and other citizens. By mutual agreement it was established that the Great and General Council would delegate its powers to a Council of State formed by the following people: the two Captains Regent, ten members of the current Council, the Special Delegate, the two Secretaries of State and five members, chosen among the citizens not belonging to the Council, appointed by the Captains Regent."*[84]

Between the two sessions of the Parliament, something happened that accelerated the plans to form a super-government that would help the country overcome that grave moment.

---

82. Ibid.

83. Gildo Gasperoni – *Itinerario Politico: a San Marino e in Europa in difesa della democrazia* (Political itinerary: in San Marino and Europe in defense of democracy) – A.I.EP. Editrice, 1983, RSM.

84. From the minutes of the Great and General Council, session held on October 28, 1943 – State Archives of the Republic of San Marino.

ROMMEL'S ARRIVAL

In those days, the Gothic Line was being drawn. The initial hypothesis was that the long trench would start in Rimini and end in Massa Carrara, passing through San Marino. Mount Titano served as a significant defensive stronghold, so on October 25, Field Marshal Erwin Rommel, better known as "the Desert Fox, "visited the location. He was received with all the honors. The people of San Marino certainly could not waste an opportunity like that. This important officer's visit reaffirmed that San Marino had always been a loyal friend of Germany and a neutral state. They firmly requested that this neutrality be respected by the German army. Rommel then asked to personally inspect the military equipment of the small Republic, ascertaining that San Marino possessed four Italian cannons donated by King Vittorio Emanuele III in 1907, of which only two were functional and were used solely to fire blanks during official celebrations.

The infantry weapons consisted of 80 model 1891 Carcano rifles, remnants of the First World War, along with two boxes of bullets, also dating back to WWI.[85] After witnessing the weaponry available to the smallest Republic in the world, which could barely frighten the pigeons perched on the local Statue of Liberty, Rommel requested to sign the "Golden Book" dedicated to distinguished guests and personally assured that the neutrality of San Marino would not be violated by Nazi Germany. He then had the Gothic line redrawn to

85. Mimmo Franzinelli, *RSI – La Repubblica del Duce 1943-1945* (RSI – the Duce's Republic 1943-1945), Mondadori, 2007, Milan (pag. 6).

exclude the small country from that terrible trench, moving the starting point further south; the line would now begin in Pesaro instead of Rimini.

October 28, 1943, was a day that the people of San Marino experienced with great joy. Not everyone, though; for example, Giuliano Gozi was not very happy. That day, Ezio Balducci returned after nine years of exile. He was immediately appointed "Special Delegate with the belligerent armies." During his years in Rome, he had gained a level of esteem and many acquaintances in the Fascist political circles, like nobody else in San Marino at that time. Among these acquaintances were Alessandro Pavolini, the newly appointed secretary of the Fascist Republican Party, and Marshal Rodolfo Graziani, with whom Balducci had fought side by side in Africa during the war. On December 10, 1943, Balducci wrote in a letter to his friend Adami[86] that Mussolini himself had requested his return to San Marino as well as his role as Special Delegate.[87]

Balducci got to work immediately. His first step was to check the status of essential goods stocks in the government depots because the unexpected was looming. The 7,000 refugees present at that time in San Marino were not only well-received, but they also became an invaluable source of income for many local inhabitants. Yet, the predictions about the approaching front, as everyone had discovered by then, led people to believe that the worst was yet to come.

By sheer coincidence, another individual arrived on Mount Titano alongside Balducci. An alarming phone call was received at the Public Palace: *"A car with a German license plate has just crossed the border in Dogana. It must be a big shot. The car has wheels without spokes."*[88]

---

86. Lieutenant Adriano Adami, born in Perugia in 1921, Monterosa Division, 1st Regiment of Bassano Battalion, sentenced to death by a people's court on May 5, 1945.

87. Ezio Balducci archive – envelope no. 2, letter dated December 10, 1943, State Archives, RSM.

88. Lieutenant Adriano Adami, born in Perugia in 1921, Monterosa Division, 1st Regiment of Bassano Battalion, sentenced to death by a people's court on May 5, 1945.

The border official did not know that hubcaps, which covered the rims on new model cars, had been invented. In a flash, the government leaders prepared to welcome this mysterious figure with pomp and circumstance. After about a quarter of an hour, the car with a diplomatic license plate pulled up in the main square, Liberty Square. The Palace guard quickly adjusted the sleeves of his uniform and opened the main door to the Palace, as was customary for government authorities. Some people were peeking out of the Public Palace to see who had arrived. The rear door of the car opened, but that mysterious man, who was almost two meters tall, instead of heading towards them, went the other way... towards the post office, leaving everyone with their mouths wide open!

After several minutes of agitation inside the Palace, someone mustered the courage to cross the square and walk into the post office. He walked right up to the man who was calmly buying some stamps for his collection and said, "Excuse me, Sir, is that car out there yours?" "Of course! Nice to meet you, my name is Gumpert."

Gerhard Richard Gumpert was born in 1910 in Kahla. After graduating from law school, he began a diplomatic career at the German embassies in Spain, Belgium, Finland, and Turkey. In 1940, he was appointed Secretary of Legation at the Embassy in Rome. In July 1943, he had to return home for his father's funeral. During his trip back from Germany, he was detained in Tuscany for a few days due to the turmoil caused by the fall of Fascism. When he finally arrived in Rome, he found the Embassy closed. Only a cook and his driver remained there; all the others had gone away.[89]

However, a long line was waiting at the front door of the Embassy. Gumpert, without losing heart or wondering why all his colleagues had left that place, decided to reopen the Embassy and work there alone. Some people, disappointed by the fall of Fascism, requested visas to emigrate to Germany; others asked to send parcels to relatives who were prisoners in Nazi concentration camps. Gumpert

89. From the interview with Carl Fredric Marino Gumpert, son of Gerard Richard Gumpert, dated December 18, 2010, RSM.

tried to please everyone. He also managed to send a large number of railway wagons loaded with goods to the prisoners. This action earned him a Medal of Merit from the Italian Red Cross, even though it seems that all those goods were given to the German civilian population once they arrived there. After the events that occurred on September 8th, Gumpert learned of Kappler's intention to retaliate against Italian civilians, who from that moment on were considered traitors of the Reich. He also knew about the imminent deportation of Jews to Nazi concentration camps. Thus, he played a part that went down in history. He wrote a letter whose contents were entirely fabricated. Pretending to be the "Pope," he asked Hitler not to implement any acts of repression on either the civilian population or the Jews in Rome; otherwise, he would take a tough stance against Germany. Then, he asked his friend, the former Apostolic Nuncio to Czechoslovakia, to transcribe the text on headed paper from the Vatican and then return it to him, all done secretly, of course. Gumpert then enclosed this letter in an envelope containing another letter written by himself, stating he had a meeting with the Holy Father and that he had been given that message to relay. He sent the envelope to Joachim Von Ribbentrop, the German Foreign Minister.

Hitler never discovered that there was another "Pope" in Rome. However, he did learn that an Embassy, which had been officially closed, was still open; therefore, Gumpert was ordered to go immediately to the new Embassy in Fasano del Garda.

He left for Fasano with his driver, the cook, and all her pots and pans. He decided to drive along the Adriatic coast rather than through Tuscany. When he arrived in Rimini, he saw Mount Titano to his left. He recognized its profile and immediately decided to take a small detour to buy some stamps.[90]

"You see, we are having a bit of trouble, could you give us a hand?" he was told at the post office. This is how his great friendship with San Marino began. Historian Amedeo Montemaggi said: *"Gumpert*

90. From the interview with Carl Fredric Marino Gumpert, son of Gerard Richard Gumpert, dated December 18, 2010, RSM.

On the right, the German Ambassador Rudolph Rahn, in the middle Gerard Richard Gumpert. (Gothic Line Archives, Rimini.)

helped the small Republic during its hard times more than anyone else." That stopover, which initially was supposed to last a few minutes, went on for several days.[91]

All Saints' Day of 1943 will never be forgotten in Rimini. On that November 1, at noon, the air-raid siren sounded. Almost immediately, a squadron of Allied four-engine planes arrived from the sea, and the first of the 372 bombs that hit the city began to fall. Those who were there remembered that the air vibrated with the sound of the flying fortresses, but very few of the 40,000 citizens of Rimini were frightened by the sirens; they were accustomed to warplanes flying by. It did not even occur to them that the Allied troops had chosen their city to enter the Po Valley, and for that precise reason it had to be burned to the ground. That day, the seaside town counted 68 dead; there were chasms in the streets and gardens, some of which were even up to five meters deep, as remembered by the witnesses.[92]

---

91. From the interview with Amedeo Montemaggi, Rimini.

92. Fabio Glauco Galli - *La città invisibile, segni, storie e memorie di pace pane e guerra* (The invisible city, signs, stories and recollections about peace, bread and war), Edizioni Fulmino, Savignano sul Rubicone (FC) 2009.

The explosions were clearly heard even from San Marino, where the people, in disbelief, watched what was happening just a hop and a skip away from them. Before night fell, the first groups of refugees began to climb up Mount Titano in search of a safe haven. Soon after, it became an endless caravan of people that would not end until September 1944.

On November 3rd, Ezio Balducci visited Predappio, Benito Mussolini's birthplace, where the Duce was making an appearance. Balducci brought with him the first report he had just prepared on food stocks in San Marino and a list of requests regarding some missing goods. He also discussed with Mussolini an idea he had: creating a Republican Fascist Party in San Marino, similar to the one in the Republic of Salò, to quell the heated German sentiments that had caused significant trouble the previous month.[93]

But the wave of people seeking shelter in that minute territory did not cease for one moment. Moreover, winter was approaching. The Commission of the public body responsible for inspecting ration books created a new list of urgently needed goods.[94]

On the morning of November 12, Balducci went to Rimini with Paolo Tacchi, the Secretary of the Fascist Republican Party of that city. There, they met the leaders of the local German command. The meeting had moments of tension, especially when the Germans criticized San Marino for its lack of supervision of the blackout measures at night. In particular, they protested against a factory in Chiesanuova, where strange movements had been observed at night. Then, the discussion shifted to the Jewish problem. According to the Germans, some Jews had been hiding on Mount Titano. Balducci denied this vigorously, after which Paolo Tacchi spoke. Although he had always faced accusations of making several incursions into the territory of San Marino, this time he gave his word that no Jews were present

93. Ezio Balducci Archive – letter dated November 3, 1943, envelope no. 2, file no. 5, State Archives, RSM.

94. Ezio Balducci Archive – letter dated November 11, 1943, State Archives, RSM.

there. He knew very well that there was no truth in his statements, yet he managed, at least on that occasion, to convince his accusers.[95]

This fact was revealed a few years later, when, at the court of Forlì, Ezio Balducci was called as a witness in the trial where Tacchi was accused of murdering three martyrs in Rimini. All this was repeated, in the same form and concept, in an interview given by Tacchi himself to Professor Amedeo Montemaggi in 1964. But what had actually happened that morning?

That meeting did take place! This was confirmed by Balducci himself in a letter sent to the Captains Regent that same day.

On November 12, he reported in full detail what he had been asked by the German command. He quoted in his third point: "*The German Command strongly urges the Government of the Republic not to give shelter to Jews of any nationality.*"[96]

Then, he informed the Heads of State that a committee had been established in Rimini to assist the victims of the bombings. Balducci ended his letter by writing: "*I think that a fair offer from the Republic would be very welcome and significant to confirm the solidarity given to the victims of the bombings.*"

Assuming that the request for an offer was morally correct, the term "fair" is quite ambiguous. Balducci himself was working diligently to determine what was most needed for the survival of San Marino's growing population during those days. The same day, he wrote a letter to Teodoro Lonfernini instructing him to go and exchange an undefined amount of German marks, some of which were in a non-convertible currency. Lonfernini would have to go to the Banca d'Italia in Rimini to cash in on those marks.[97] A consideration should be made at this point: it is rather difficult to imagine where that money came from. However, returning to the request made by

---

95. From the interview with Amedeo Montemaggi, Rimini "*(...) he said that to me during an interview in 1964, here at my home (...)*".

96. Ezio Balducci Archive – letter dated November 12, 1943, State Archives, RSM.

97. Ezio Balducci Archive – letter to Teodoro Lonfernini dated November 12, 1943, State Archives, RSM.

REPUBBLICA  DI S. MARINO

CITTADINI !

La Patria attraversa un momento estremamente difficile e pericoloso; occorre perciò che ogni buon cittadino, senza raccogliere notizie allarmistiche, senza diffondere voci catastrofiche, abbia piena fiducia nell'opera del Governo, che nulla lascia intentato per salvaguardare la sovranità della Repubblica.

Potrebbe nondimeno accadere che questa dovesse subire la sorte di uno stato minuscolo e indifeso coinvolto suo malgrado nel vortice di una guerra non sua, ed allora ai Sammarinesi sarà duopo di maggiore coraggio e di maggiore fiducia.

Agli sfollati, che per sottrarsi al furore dei bombardamenti nelle vicine città, si sono quassù rifugiati, confidando nella incolumità della Repubblica ospitale, la Reggenza rivolge caldo appello perchè si mostrino più che mai consapevoli dei doveri che loro si impongono, e perchè non accrescano le difficoltà del momento.

Tutti diano esempio di fermezza e di disciplina, mentre il Governo rimane al suo posto di lavoro e di lotta contro il minacciar degli eventi, confidando nella virtù che lo regge e nel patrocinio del Santo, che sempre nei frangenti più minacciosi, protesse e salvò l'integrità della Patria.

Viva la Repubblica di S. Marino!

San Marino, 31 Luglio 1944-1643 d. F. R.

The Captains Regent invite citizens and refugees to have confidence in the Government's work during the trying times ahead.
— Courtesy of the State Archives of the Republic of San Marino. —

the Special Delegate to the Captains Regent, it must be noted that this was not in line with the logic of the actions that had always distinguished Ezio Balducci in all his activities. It would be more consistent to consider it a bribe or, better yet, a "gift" to make the officer who had actually made that request forget all about it. This is obviously a guess. However, it is to be noted that a few days before, Ugo Ughi, the Mayor of Rimini, had succeeded Eugenio Bianchini thanks to an intervention by Tacchi, who included him among his most faithful collaborators. On the days that followed, Ughi turned to Balducci and obtained a comfortable, safe haven in San Marino for his whole family.[98] Paolo Tacchi, instead, "modestly" asked to be granted the house of the "Jewish Malagola."[99] However, this request was not accepted, firstly because Malagola was not a Jew, and also because the house had already been sold to the Neris from Forlì some time before. From these requests, it seems that those people were trying to obtain favors from Balducci, which were far from being legal, rather than having a relationship of friendship and collaboration.

The case originating from the meeting on November 12, 1943, would end, at least officially, with the letter sent by the Secretary for Home Affairs to the Political Inspector dated November 22. The Minister ordered Pietro Animali to patrol the area carefully so that "*individuals of the Jewish race*" would not settle down within the territory of San Marino.

Clearly, that document was written to demonstrate that San Marino was also enforcing the race laws mandated by the Nazis. However, it is now widely recognized that the truth was precisely the opposite of what everyone insisted on trying to prove.

---

98. Ezio Balducci Archive – letter by Ugo Ughi dated January 8, 1944, State Archives, RSM.

99. Ezio Balducci Archive – letter by Paolo Tacchi dated January 4, 1944, State Archives, RSM.

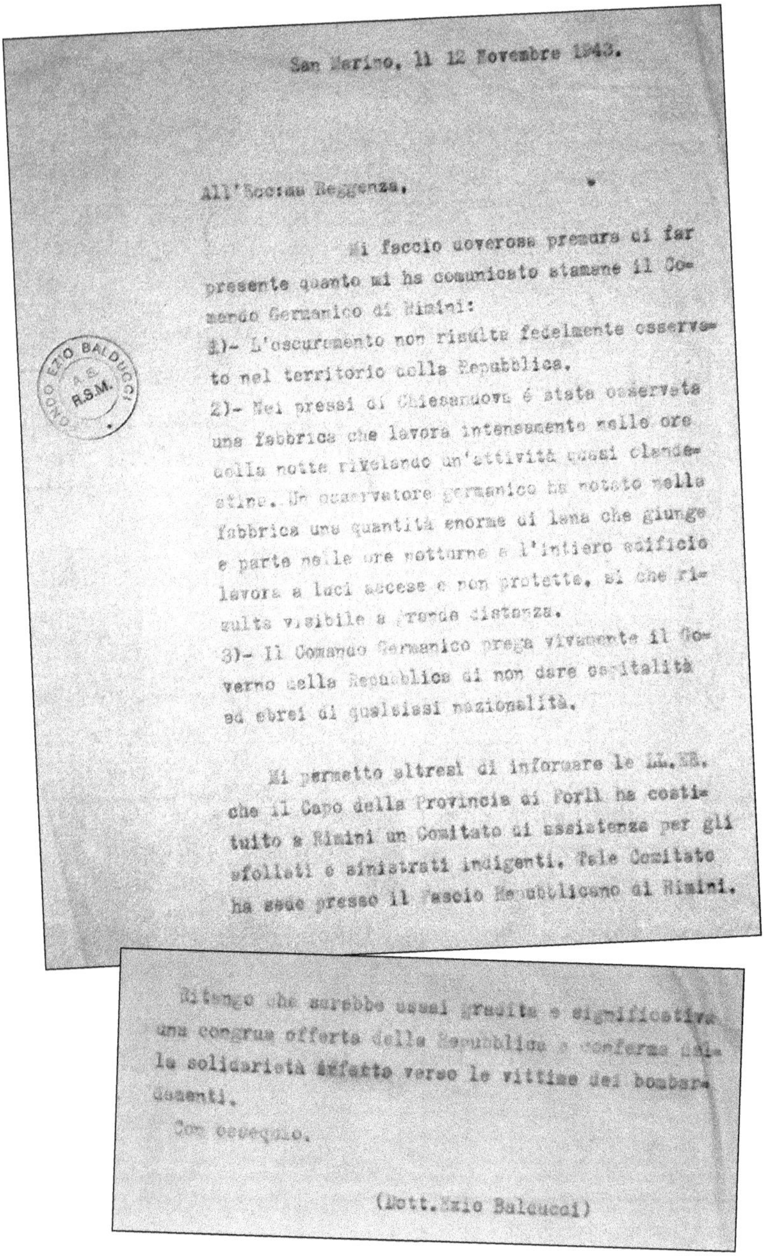

San Marino, lì 12 Novembre 1943.

All'Eccrma Reggenza,

Mi faccio doverosa premura di far presente quanto mi ha comunicato stamane il Comando Germanico di Rimini:

1)- L'oscuramento non risulta fedelmente osservato nel territorio della Repubblica.

2)- Nei pressi di Chiesanuova é stata osservata una fabbrica che lavora intensamente nelle ore della notte rivelando un'attività quasi clandestina. Un osservatore germanico ha notato nella fabbrica una quantità enorme di lana che giunge e parte nelle ore notturne e l'intiero edificio lavora a luci accese e non protette, sì che risulta visibile a grande distanza.

3)- Il Comando Germanico prega vivamente il Governo della Repubblica di non dare ospitalità ad ebrei di qualsiasi nazionalità.

Mi permetto altresì di informare le LL.EE. che il Capo della Provincia di Forlì ha costituito a Rimini un Comitato di assistenza per gli sfollati e sinistrati indigenti. Tale Comitato ha sede presso il Fascio Repubblicano di Rimini.

Ritengo che sarebbe assai gradita e significativa una congrua offerta della Repubblica a conferma della solidarietà affetto verso le vittime dei bombardamenti.

Con ossequio.

(Dott. Ezio Balducci)

Front and back of a letter sent to the Captains Regent by Ezio Balducci on November 12, 1943.
— Courtesy of the State Archives of the Republic of San Marino. —

San Marino November 12, 1943

To Their Excellencies, the Captains Regent

I hereby inform you what the German Command in Rimini has communicated to me this morning:

1)- blackout measures are not fully complied with within the territory of the Republic.

2)- in the vicinity of the town of Chiesanuova a factory has been seen working intensely during the night, as if it were carrying out some clandestine activities. A German observer has noticed a huge quantity of wool coming and going during the night. The whole building works with the lights on and unprotected, so it is perfectly visible from a distance.

3)- the German Command firmly requests the government of the Republic not to give hospitality to Jews of any nationality.

Please be also informed that the Head of the Province of Forlì has created a Committee for displaced people and victims in need in Rimini. This Committee is housed at the Republican Fascist Offices in Rimini.

I think that a fair offer from the Republic would be very welcomed and significant to confirm the solidarity given to the victims of the bombings.

Yours sincerely,

(Dr. Ezio Balducci)
THE SECRETARY OF STATE
for Home Affairs

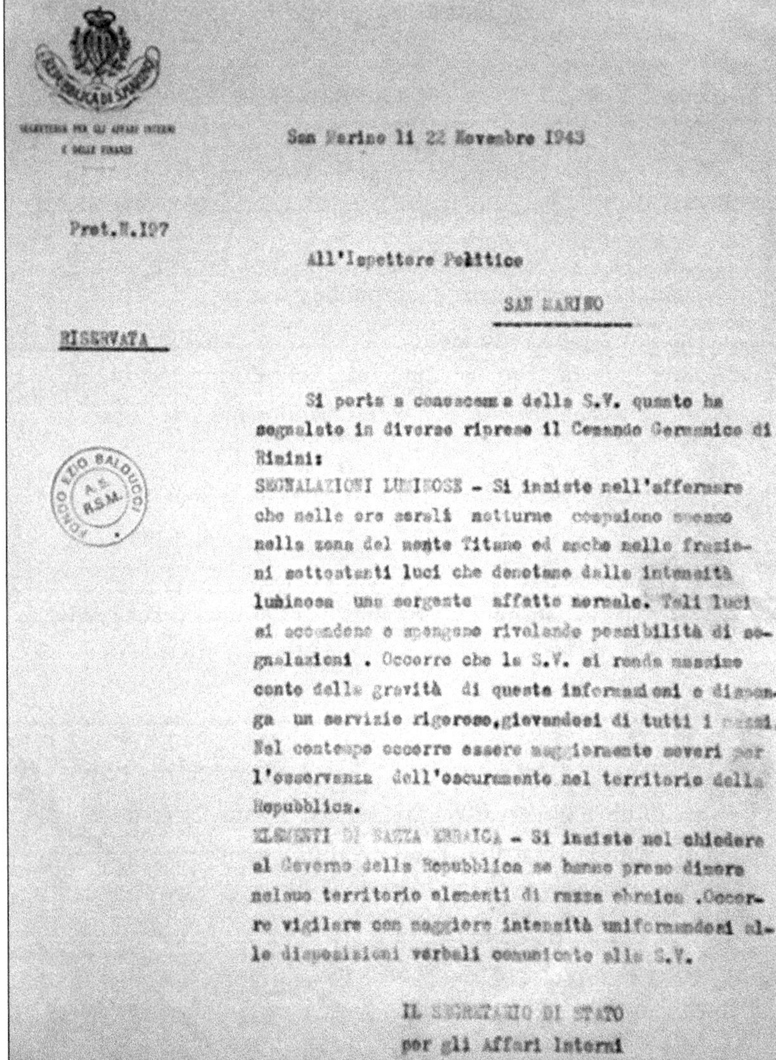

SEGRETERIA PER GLI AFFARI INTERNI E DELLE FINANZE

San Marino li 22 Novembre 1943

Prot.N.197

All'Ispettore Politico

SAN MARINO

RISERVATA

Si porta a conoscenza della S.V. quanto ha segnalato in diverse riprese il Comando Germanico di Rimini:

SEGNALAZIONI LUMINOSE - Si insiste nell'affermare che nelle ore serali notturne compaiono spesso nella zona del monte Titano ed anche nelle frazioni sottostanti luci che denotano dalla intensità luminosa una sorgente affatto normale. Tali luci si accendono e spengono rivelando possibilità di segnalazioni . Occorre che la S.V. si renda massimo conto della gravità di queste informazioni e disponga un servizio rigoroso, giovandosi di tutti i mezzi. Nel contempo occorre essere maggiormente severi per l'osservanza dell'oscuramento nel territorio della Repubblica.

ELEMENTI DI RAZZA EBRAICA - Si insiste nel chiedere al Governo della Repubblica se hanno preso dimora nel suo territorio elementi di razza ebraica .Occorre vigilare con maggiore intensità uniformandosi alle disposizioni verbali comunicate alla S.V.

IL SEGRETARIO DI STATO
per gli Affari Interni

Letter dated November 22, 1943.
— Courtesy of the State Archives of the Republic of San Marino. —

San Marino, November 22, 1943

File No. 197

To the Political Inspector
SAN MARINO

CONFIDENTIAL

Please be informed about what has been repeatedly communicated by the German Command in Rimini:

ILLUMINATED SIGNALS – it is once again stated that lights have been observed in the area of Mount Titano and the surrounding neighborhood during the evening hours. These lights are certainly not normal. They flicker on and off, indicating possible signaling. You are urged to regard this serious information with the highest consideration and to organize thorough patrols using every resource at your disposal.

Moreover, you must pay strict attention to enforcing the observance of blackout measures within the territory of the Republic.

INDIVIDUALS BELONGING TO THE JEWISH RACE – we hereby insist on asking the government of the Republic whether individuals belonging to the Jewish race are living within the territory of San Marino or not. You have to monitor the situation more carefully to comply with the verbal orders you have been given.

THE SECRETARY OF STATE
for Internal Affairs.

While the Government of San Marino was working hard to store as many essential goods as possible — on November 16, another devastating bombing hit Rimini, dramatically increasing the number of displaced people heading to San Marino — something else must surely have happened. It might have been an informer, eager to do some business, who had squealed. Or maybe a spy for the Nazis who was hidden among the thousands of people who had flocked to that peaceful Republic? No one knows for sure! But on December 13, the Secretary of State for Foreign Affairs received an urgent confidential letter from the Consul of the Italian Social Republic, Vincenzo Guglielmi. He asked him for the list of people belonging to the Jewish race. From a first reading, you may notice that it was hastily written. In fact, the Consul stated that "every Jew must be considered as belonging to a country at war with the Republic of Italy". If the writer had been more careful and clearer-headed, he would have written: "with the Italian Social Republic". Apart from formalities, the list of all the Jewish people was requested again on that day along with the names of those who were married to them, even if they were of the Aryan race. These lists would be compared with the ones deposited at the Consulate.

But which list did Consul Guglielmi have? Was the name of Camillo Castiglioni, with whom he had spent hour after hour pleasantly playing cards, on that list? Or was the Mandelli family, where he had occasionally gone to dinner, on it? Was he angry about that time when he had been invited to their home to have roast beef, but ended up settling for two eggs because some stray cats had snuck into the kitchen and eaten the roast beef a few minutes before dinner?[100]

Certainly, Vincenzo Guglielmi knew many of the Jews who lived in San Marino. Was he trying to blackmail someone to earn extra money, or had he truly received an urgent request from the Social Republic? Or had he been ordered by the Germans, who dominated the Republic of Salò, to deliver an official document that once again

100. From the interview with Maria José Mandelli, Reggio Calabria.

Ezio Balducci.
— Courtesy of the State Archives of the Republic of San Marino. —

proved to Hitler and his henchmen that San Marino was a model to be followed in the implementation of racial policies?

Along with the letter filed in the registry under no. 1420, the Consulate also sent a request, logged as no. 1421, for the list of draft dodgers.

Then, something strange, or at least unusual, happened. Balducci had truly been frightened by the previous request received in Rimini, but this time it seemed that he couldn't care less about it. Exactly three days after that extremely dangerous threat — if a letter written hastily and arrogantly from a diplomatic point of view can be defined as a threat — Balducci moved Hans Wetzlar, another Jew under surveillance, to San Marino.

Hans Wetzlar was of German origin. Eight years earlier, he had moved to Italy, married Graziella, and had a daughter together. He lost his original nationality and consequently became stateless, as he could not obtain Italian citizenship because he was a Jew. Wetzlar had been hospitalized for 25 days at the "Villa Salus" clinic in Viserbella di Rimini due to a rare form of chronic enterocolitis of bacillary origin. There, he was guarded by the police. He decided to turn to Paolo Tacchi and Balducci, whom he knew very well, for help in finding a safe hiding place in case of deportation.

RISERVATA-URGENTE N.1420

Consolato d'Italia
in San Marino

Ill.mo
Signor Segretario di Stato
per gli Affari Esteri della Repubblica
di
S A N M A R I N O

San Marino 13 dicembre 1943,XXII.

(Oggetto) Appartenenti a razza ebraica .

(Testo) Per poter corrispondere ad analoga urgente richiesta del mio Governo e confrontare nel contempo i relativi dati con quelli in possesso di questo Consolato,prego la cortesia della S.V.I. favorire l'elenco,aggiornato con le complete generalità di ciascuna,di tutte le persone di nazionalità italiana-originaria od acquisita-residenti nel territorio della Vostra Repubblica,appartenenti a razza ebraica,anche se coniugate con persone di razza ariana.

Con l'occasione la S.V.I. vorrà essere cortese rendere noto a questo Consolato se e quali provvedimenti si intende di adottare da parte del Governo di San Marino in relazione alla recente norma italiana in base alla quale ogni ebreo è considerato come appartenente a paese in guerra con la Repubblica d'Italia.

In attesa,vogliate gradire le espressioni della più distinta considerazione.

IL CONSOLE D'ITALIA
(F.°) Guglielmi

CONFIDENTIAL - URGENT No. 1420

CONSULATE OF ITALY
IN SAN MARINO

To
The Secretary of State
for Foreign Affairs of the Republic
of
SAN MARINO

San Marino, December 13, 1943, XXII

(Subject) People Belonging to the Jewish Race

(Text) To fulfill a similar urgent request from my government and to compare your records with those held by this Consulate, I kindly ask that you send me the updated list detailing the full personal information of each individual of original or acquired Italian nationality residing within the territory of the Republic of San Marino and belonging to the Jewish race, even if married to individuals of the Aryan race.

Please be so kind as to inform this Consulate about the measures, if any, which will be taken by the government of San Marino concerning the recent Italian legislation according to which every Jew is considered as a person belonging to a country at war with the Republic of Italy.

Yours sincerely,

THE CONSUL OF ITALY
(Signed) Guglielmi

Then, on January 12, 1944, exactly one month after receiving those letters, the Government sent a bizarre reply to Consul Guglielmi. The Italian diplomat was informed that San Marino had given precise instructions not to grant asylum to any Jews. Nothing strange so far. However, the letter went on to state that after a meeting with the head of the province of Forlì, the rules had changed: Jewish women married to Italian Aryan citizens were no longer to be considered Jewish. What was occurring in San Marino? There are two possibilities: either San Marino had misunderstood the situation, or they were trying to pull the Consul's leg.

Indeed, it is true that the original laws written in Nuremberg stated this precisely. However, since March 1943, Hitler also began to deport Catholics married to Jews without making any distinction, and he imposed this action on other countries as well.[101] The Grünfelds were a perfect example of this. Maria José Mandelli reported that after the war, they learned that a cousin of her mother's, who lived in Paris and was married to a Catholic, had been captured with her husband during a raid. They had both been deported to a concentration camp, where her husband had been killed immediately. She had been saved by the fact that she spoke six languages and was assigned the role of interpreter inside the camp. She had returned home only after the war, walking across the whole of Germany.

So, the question remains the same: what was going on? To get a clearer view, you have to read the speech given by Ezio Balducci to the Great and General Council during the last session before the Christmas holidays. He attacked the members of Parliament one by one. They were all guilty of misconduct, or those who were not had kept quiet while aware of what the others were doing. Some had taken advantage of the displaced people, making them pay higher rents

101. Mimmo Franzinelli, quoted work, pp.8 (quotation from the letters by the GNR cadets "Ermanno Migliarini, in Italy there are still groups of races which are too different and inferior to ours. In particular, they are Jews or men who have often linked their existence, even unconsciously, to Jewish interests; our policy towards them shall be merciless. There is only one possible way to follow: their complete extermination").

than they should, others had done business on the black market, and most had packed away goods controlled by the public body deputed to the inspection of ration books. Those who had not personally done any of these things had friends or relatives who had! In short, Balducci crucified each one of them. And as icing on the cake, he added the letters received from Consul Guglielmi to his accusations

But if you look carefully at these letters and compare them with the reply, you can notice a few peculiar details: the letters sent by the Consulate are not signed! They are, in fact, the carbon copy of the original documents. But what was a copy of the Consulate archive doing in Balducci's files? Another detail that really stands out is the typewriter used to write the reply: it has the same defects as the one used to type the requests. So, what was going on? It is very simple: Ezio Balducci had generated the greatest farce in the history of San Marino! After the consultation with Mussolini on November 3, 1943, the "Republican Fascist Government of San Marino" was officially created on January 4, 1944. However, upon closer inspection, this government had very little to do with being Fascist: out of the twenty members, only five could be defined as having a real Fascist ideology. Just an example of this: Augusto Foschi, who was also a member of Ermenegildo Gasperoni's clandestine Communist Party, joined this new Government. Giuliano Gozi had been appointed Secretary of the newly born party. He accepted this position, saying, *"[I'm doing it] just for the sake of the country and to prevent possible incursions by the Fascists of Rimini."*[102] Balducci had to convince everybody in San Marino about the risks they were running. He used every means possible to do this, including cleverness, astuteness, and that insane amount of courage of which he had such a great quantity!

---

102. Ezio Balducci Archive, document dated November 9, 1943, envelope no. 2, file no. 5, State Archives, RSM.

San Marino li 15 Dicembre 1943

Carissimo Comm. Cima ,

In ossequio al Vostro gentile consiglio viene a Voi HANS WETHZAR per documentarvi la propria posizione. La delicatezza dell'argomento e del momento non avrebbe consentito a me ed a Tacchi l'interessamento che portiamo al caso presente se, alla luce degli stessi certificati, non presentasse degli estremi che meritano una coscienziosa attenzione.

Se a tale fatto si aggiungono le considerazioni relative al contegno e alle doti personali del Wethzar che da tanto tempo vive a Rimini e gode l'affettuosa simpatia di quanti lo avvicinano, viene maggiormente confortata la sua speranza di non essere interiormente incluso nella Lista degli appartenenti alla razza ebraica .

Con tanti ringraziamenti e cordiali saluti

(Dott. Ezio Balducci)

A letter about Hans Wetzlar's case by Ezio Balducci dated December 15, 1493.
— Courtesy of the State Archives of the Republic of San Marino. —

Regina Grymberg Brambilla sent a greeting card to Ezio Balducci.
— Courtesy of the State Archives of the Republic of San Marino. —

San Marino, December 15, 1943

Dear Commander Cima,

Following your kind advice, Mr. Hans Wetzlar will be visiting you to explain his position to you. Considering the extremely delicate matter and period, it would not be possible for me and Tacchi to dedicate our total interest to this case if, in light of these certificates, elements that deserve thorough attention are not submitted.

If to the above stated we add the considerations about Wetzlar's behavior and personal qualities, besides the fact that he has been living in Rimini for such a long time and is loved by all those who know him, his hope of not being included in the list of the people belonging to the Jewish race is even more strengthened.

Many thanks. Yours sincerely,

(Dr. Ezio Balducci)

To: Dr. Ezio Balducci,
Serravalle

1943-1944

From Regina Brambilla

I wish you a Merry Christmas and a Happy New Year with my fondest gratitude.

N.° 800.

San Marino li 12 Gennaio 1944/1643 d.F.R.

Al Signor
Console d'Italia in
SAN MARINO

In merito alla nota N. 1421 della S.V. e a conferma delle mie dichiarazioni verbali, comunico che ho dato da qualche tempo istruzioni all'Ispettorato Politico perchè non conceda permessi di soggiorno su questo territorio a cittadini italiani obbligati al servizio militare che non siano provvisti di regolari documenti dell'Autorità Militare.

Il mio Governo desidera che l'opportuno controllo sulla regolarità della posizione militare dei cittadini italiani qui trasferitisi, sia fatto dal Consolato Italiano, per naturale competenza: e poichè tale controllo dovrebbe essere preventivo, così ordinerei che l'Ispettorato Politico non rilasci permessi di soggiorno a questa categoria di cittadini, se il documento militare non porta il visto del Consolato.

L'elenco dei militari quì residenti in congedo è in via di informazione e appena sarà pronto Le verrà rimesso.

Per quanto riguarda la chiamata alle armi delle classi, l'Ispettorato mi fa presente che nelle attuali contingenze sarebbe opportuno che gli obbligati fossero invitati a presentarsi a cotesto Consolato.

A carico degli inadempienti alla chiamata alle armi, e a carico dei cittadini italiani soggetti a servizio militare che sprovvisti di permesso di soggiorno, quì avessero preso dimora, il Governo applicherà le disposizioni dell'art. 40 della Convenzione 31 Marzo 1939.

In merito alla nota N° 1420 della S.V. il Governo è stato informato dall'Eccellenza il Capo della Provincia di Forlì, di nuovi provvedimenti riguardanti gli appartenenti alla razza ebraica, in forza dei quali le donne di tale razza coniugate con ariani italiani, sarebbero esenti dalle misure in precedenza stabilite.

Per intanto, da parte nostra sono stati dati ordini precisi di non accordare il permesso di soggiorno alle persone appartenenti a razza ebraica.

Siccome il Governo intende anche in questo campo di esaminare i provvedimenti da prendere in relazione a quelli già deliberati dal Governo italiano, così La prego di volere procurarsi il testo delle nuove disposizioni in oggetto per una cortese comunicazione a questa Segreteria.

./.

First page of a letter dated January 12, 1944.

— Courtesy of the State Archives of the Republic of San Marino; Ezio Balducci Archive. —

No. 300.
San Marino, January 12, 1944/1643 d.F.R.[103]
To the Consul of Italy in SAN MARINO

With regards to your note no. 1421 and as a confirmation of my verbal statements, please be informed that some time ago I gave instructions to the Political Inspectorate not to grant residence permits, within this territory, to Italian citizens with military service obligations who do not have valid documents issued by the military authority.

My government requests that appropriate control of the regularity of the military position of Italian citizens who have moved here is made by the Italian Consulate, as it is their concern. And since this monitoring should be preventive, I would order the Political Inspectorate not to issue any residence permits to this category of citizens should their military documents not be stamped by the Consulate.

The list of the soldiers on leave residing in San Marino is being processed and I will send it to you as soon as it is ready.

As for the call to arms of the classes, the Inspectorate has pointed out that in the current situation, it would be helpful if the men due to enroll came to this Consulate.

The provisions of Art. 40 of the Convention dated March 31, 1939, will be applied against those who have not fulfilled their call to arms and the Italian citizens serving in the army who are residing here without a permit.

As for your note no. 1420, the government has been informed by the Head of the Province of Forlì that new measures concerning the Jews have been implemented. According to such provisions, the women belonging to that race married to Aryan Italians are exempt from the measures previously established.

In the meantime, we have given strict orders not to grant residence permits to people belonging to the Jewish race.

103. d.F.R. stands for "Since the Foundation of the Republic". It is a formula to refer to dates which is still used today in official documents [translator's note].

Come Le esposi verbalmente, sono di prossima istituzione a San Marino una sezione autonoma annonaria e un ufficio di assistenza per gli sfollati che saranno diretti dall'Autorità Comunale di Rimini.

Quell'Autorità Comunale prenderà con la S.V. gli opportuni accordi a riguardo di queste nuove istituzioni.

Voi più deferenti saluti.

IL SEGRETARIO DI STATO

Second page of a letter dated January 12, 1944.

— Courtesy of the State Archives of the Republic of San Marino; Ezio Balducci Archive. —

As the government of San Marino wants to examine the measures to be taken in accordance with those already approved by the Italian government, I kindly ask you to send the text of any new provisions in this sector to this Secretariat.

As I told you verbally, an autonomous section deputed to the control of stocks and an office for assistance to displaced people will soon be established in San Marino under the direction of the municipality of Rimini.

That authority will make the appropriate arrangements with you for what concerns these new institutions.

With the most respectful regards.

THE SECRETARY OF STATE

THE REPUBLICAN FASCIST GOVERNMENT OF SAN MARINO

On that same date, January 4, 1944, in the Italian Social Republic, the head of the General Inspectorate of Race, Giovanni Preziosi, a close friend of Hitler and Rosenberg, made Mussolini enact Legislative Decree no. 2, which included all the new racial provisions. He also introduced special "political and racial culture" courses for the officers of the Republican Guard.[104]

On Mount Titano, Consul Vincenzo Guglielmi was likely unaware of what Balducci was doing behind his back. Alternatively, he might have been complicit in it. Either way, he continued to play his cards in a country like no other, where war did not exist, there was an abundance of food, and the people were kind and generous. In the meantime, the Germans could still count on this friendly country... so to speak.

Yet, some were probably very frightened by that request sent "by the Consul;" many people who had favored or housed some Jews were terrified of that mysterious list in the Consul's hands. So, Balducci had to play his part once again. After sending out those false requests, he had to write a false reply as well, namely, the letter dated January 12th, just to prove that he was keeping everything under control and that the people in San Marino could sleep soundly at night.

104. Mimmo Franzinelli, quoted work.

"THE MYSTERY OF THE LETTERS"

To verify my suspicions about the letters found in the Balducci file at the State Archives of San Marino, I reached out to a typewriter collector named Italo Scaramucci. At first glance, he agreed that I might be correct, but to eliminate all doubt — and considering that he shared my fascination with the subject — he took me to Cattolica. He mentioned that there was an antique dealer in the town center who had been repairing typewriters for years. His name was Antonio Prioli, and he knew them better than anyone else.

Mr. Prioli agreed to check it out but not to make an appraisal, as I only had copies, not the original documents. In any case, he said it would take a few days. After that period, he confirmed, without any doubt, that the letters had been written by the same machine, which had to be either an Olivetti or an Everest in his opinion. However, regardless of the brand, he pointed out that in the letterhead of both letters, the letter "A" of "SAN MARINO" was slightly turned counterclockwise and was lower than the other letters; the letter "I" was clearer in the bottom right corner, meaning that the typewriter key was slightly bent backward, so less pressure was applied at that point. The same thing could be said for the letter "r," which was bent at the top left and moved to the right compared to the others. Another important detail was that when the letters "rm" were typed together, as in the words "conferma" and "norma," they were at the same "irregular" distance from each other. When overlapping the words "italiana" in the first letter and "italiano" in the second one, they matched perfectly, except, of course, for the last letter. All those defects together could not be found in two different typewriters. They were like a genetic code, according to the expert: bent keys and minor dents created by time, use, and several small incidents, such as simple grains of sand or something else, which had molded the typewriter, making it unique and one of a kind. Prioli went further, stating that the letters had been written at two different moments. In fact, between writing the first and the second one, he said, the tape had been replaced!

Those details might have gone unnoticed by all except by Antonio Prioli's expert eye.

This is how that government farce, which many took so seriously, had begun. First of all, those "*ugly mugs*" who used to run around and frighten the whole country, "*disappeared in the blink of an eye,*" said Gian Piero Gozi. They were immediately replaced, though, by that group of hotheads in black shirts, who came back again more arrogant than ever.[105] They were truly convinced that Fascism had returned to San Marino. The rulers remained silent. They might have used them as a test to gauge how far they would go, or perhaps they allowed them to carry out their raids solely to make the entire scene more credible. It must be said that they all soon joined up with the terrible "Black Brigades" in Faenza,[106] but they would come home every weekend to show their relatives and fellow citizens what great things they had learned in that school.

105. From the interview with Gian Piero Gozi, RSM.

106. Gildo Gasperoni – *Itinerario Politico: a San Marino e in Europa in difesa della democrazia* (Political itinerary: in San Marino and Europe in defense of democracy) – A.I.EP. Editrice, 1983, RSM

FONDO EZIO BALDUCCI A.S. RSM.

Viserbella, Via Brizzi 2
6 Febbraio 1944

Caro Dottor Balducci!

temo che non troverete il tempo di venire da noi prima di recarVi a Forlì e così mi permetto scriverVi quello che desideravo dirVi a voce.

Vorrei pregarVi di chiedere prima di tutto di fare abrogare il piantonamento che è stato disposto sino dal 23 Dicembre, pochi giorni dopo che con un primo ordine era stato revocato il fermo. Inoltre Vi sarei grato di chiedere al Comm. Cima il permesso di un mio trasferimento da Viserbella nell'Ospedale di San Marino. Accludo il certificato del Direttore della Casa di Cura di Viserbella che dimostra la necessità di farmi trasferire in media montagna per continuare la cura per la mia grave malattia intestinale, che mi fa soffrire da parecchi anni. Penso che il Comm. Cima non avrà nulla in contrario, dato che anche a San Marino potrà farmi vigilare. Adriana ha già fissato le camere e conta presto di andare a San Marino e Vi prego caldamente caro Dottore cercate di ottenere da Cima subito questo consenso per il mio trasferimento perché possa seguire mia moglie e bambina.

Hans Wetzlar's dramatic letter to Ezio Balducci. The first part was typed by Wetzlar himself.
— Courtesy of the State Archives of the Republic of San Marino; Ezio Balducci Archive. —

Viserbella, Via Brizzi 2

February 6, 1944

Dear Dr. Balducci,

I fear that you will not find the time to come and see us before heading to Forli, and thus please find in this letter what I wanted to discuss with you face to face.

First, I would like to request your intervention to revoke the guarding order issued on December 23rd, just a few days after my release from detention.

I would also be grateful if you could ask Commander Cima for permission for me to be transferred from Viserbella to the hospital of San Marino. I have enclosed the certificate issued by the manager of the nursing home in Viserbella, which states that I need to move to a hilly area in order to continue treatment for the serious intestinal disease that has been affecting me for many years.

I believe that Commander Cima will not object to this, since I can still be monitored even in San Marino.

Adriana has already booked the rooms and is expecting to leave for San Marino soon. I kindly ask you, dear Doctor, to try your best to obtain permission from Cima so that I can soon follow my wife and daughter.

Potete anche assicurare al Comm. Cima che non
appena il mio stato di salute me lo permetterà e
diatro un suo permesso, andrò io a Forlì e sotto-
porrò a lui un nuovo ricorso basandomi sul fatto
che sono " apolite ". Il mio grande errore è stato
di non aver mai messo in evidenza che sono " apolite
Infatti la Questura di Forlì, ufficio stranieri,
ha avuto dal Consolato Germanico di Milano già nel
Marzo l'anno scorso una comunicazione confermante
che per disposizione di legge sino dal Novembre 41
non ho più la cittadinanza germanica. Sono perciò
apolite e solo sotto questo aspetto si dovrà rie-
saminare la mia posizione giuridica ed anche razzia-
le onde ottenere la cittadinanza italiana della
quale avrei diritto, essendo sposato con una cittadina italiana ed avendo dimora fissa da 8 anni in
Italia.
Io spero tanto che con il Vostro intervento potrò
aver subito il permesso per il mio trasferimento
nell'Ospedale di San Marino, che per tante ragioni
mi sta molto al cuore. Fatemi il favore di sapermi
dire il esito del Vostro colloquio con il Comm.Cima

The second page of Wetzlar's typed letter to Balducci.
— Courtesy of the State Archives of the Republic of San Marino; Ezio Balducci Archive. —

You can also assure Commander Cima that as soon as my health allows me to do so, and after obtaining his permission, I will go to Forlì to file a new appeal based on the fact that I am "stateless." My biggest mistake is that I have never pointed out that I am "stateless". In fact, last March, the Foreign Office of the Police Headquarters of Forlì received a communication from the German Consulate in Milan confirming that, based on the law provisions dating back to November 1941, I no longer had German citizenship.

Therefore, I am stateless, and my legal and racial position must be reconsidered solely from this perspective to obtain Italian citizenship, which I am entitled to as I am married to an Italian woman and have permanently resided in Italy for eight years.

I sincerely hope that, thanks to your intervention, I will soon be able to obtain the papers for my transfer to the Hospital of San Marino, which, for many reasons, is very close to my heart. Please let me know the outcome of your meeting with Commander Cima.

frattanto Vi ringrazio infinitamente per quanto avete fatto per noi.

Cordiali saluti

Vostro [signature]

Caro Ezio

Anche ieri l'abbiamo atteso purtroppo inutilmente, le avevo preparato un magnifico dolce, conoscendolo il suo debole! - Annotti ci ha detto che era come sempre, occupatissimo, mi auguro comunque possa trovare un momento libero per venire da noi. - Come ha sentito da Ottone, ho terminato la commedia delle Sig.ne Pignotta, nella speranza che Lei così buono trovi la maniera di farci ottenere il permesso, risolvendo così la nostra penosa situazione. - Le sono infinitamente grata caro Ezio, per quanto fa per noi. La prego di perdonarmi e gradisca molti cari saluti;

The second part of Weltzar's letter to Balducci, handwritten by his wife Adriana.
— Courtesy of the State Archives of the Republic of San Marino; Ezio Balducci Archive. —

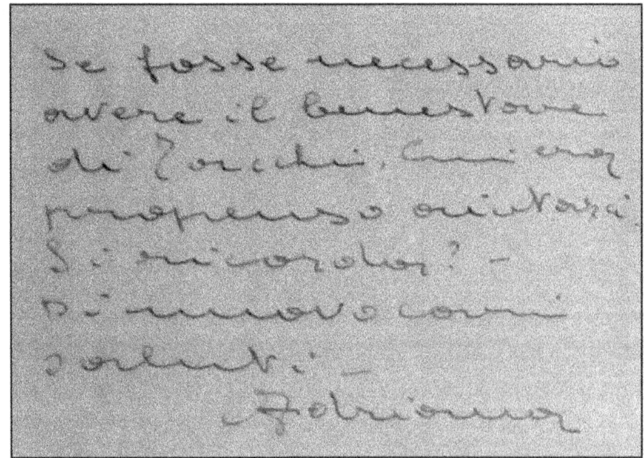

Se fosse necessario avere il benestare di Zocchi, lui era propenso aiutarci. Si ricorda? - Di nuovo cari saluti. -

Adriana

Thank you so much for all you have done for us.

Yours sincerely,

(Hans Wetzlar)

Dear Ezio,

We even waited for you yesterday, but it was in vain. I had prepared a wonderful cake, knowing your weak spot! Amati told us that you were very busy as usual; however, I hope you can find a spare moment to come and visit us. As you heard from Hans, I have booked a room at Mrs. Pignatta's house, hoping that you, who are so kind, can find a way for us to obtain permission and resolve our plight. I am infinitely grateful, dear Ezio, for everything you are doing for us. Please forgive us and receive our fondest greetings.

If it were necessary to have Tacchi's consent, he would be inclined to help us, remember?

Yours sincerely,

Adriana

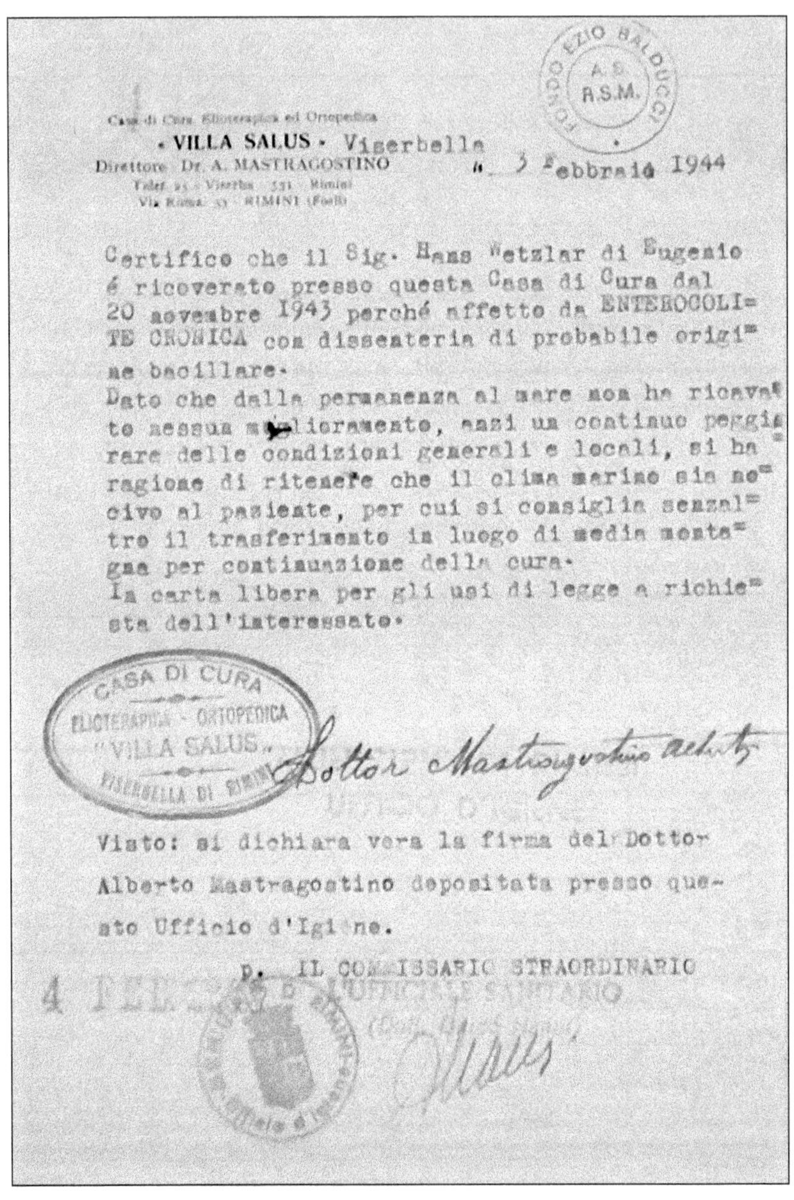

FONDO EZIO BALDUCCI A.S. R.S.M.

Casa di Cura Elioterapica ed Ortopedica
« VILLA SALUS » Viserbella
Direttore Dr. A. MASTRAGOSTINO
Telef. 25 - Viserba 531 - Rimini
Via Roma 33 - RIMINI (Forlì)

li 3 Febbraio 1944

Certifico che il Sig. Hans Wetzlar di Eugenio é ricoverato presso questa Casa di Cura dal 20 novembre 1943 perché affetto da ENTEROCOLITE CRONICA con dissenteria di probabile origine bacillare.
Dato che dalla permanenza al mare non ha ricavato nessun miglioramento, anzi un continuo peggiorare delle condizioni generali e locali, si ha ragione di ritenere che il clima marino sia nocivo al paziente, per cui si consiglia senz'altro il trasferimento in luogo di media montagna per continuazione della cura.
In carta libera per gli usi di legge a richiesta dell'interessato.

CASA DI CURA ELIOTERAPICA - ORTOPEDICA "VILLA SALUS" VISERBELLA DI RIMINI

Dottor Mastragostino Alberto

Visto: si dichiara vera la firma del Dottor Alberto Mastragostino depositata presso questo Ufficio d'Igiene.

p. IL COMMISSARIO STRAORDINARIO
L'UFFICIALE SANITARIO

Certificate prescribing to Wetzlar the transfer to a hilly area.
– State Archive, RSM, Ezio Balducci archive. –

On letter-headed paper of the "Villa Salus" Heliotherapic and Orthopaedic Nursing Home.
Manager: Dr. A. Mastragostino Viserbella, February 3, 1944
tel. 25 – Viserba 532 – Rimini
Via Roma 33 Rimini (Forlì)

I hereby certify that Mr. Hans Wetzlar, son of Eugenio Wetzlar, has been hospitalized at this nursing home since November 20, 1943, because he is afflicted with CHRONIC ENTEROCOLITIS with dysentery of probable bacillary origin.

Considering that his stay near the sea has not improved the patient's conditions, and his general and local conditions seem to have actually worsened, it is reasonably thought that this climate is unhealthy for the patient. Therefore, it is highly advisable for him to be relocated to a hilly area to continue his treatment.

This certificate is issued on non-stamped paper upon the request of the person concerned for the uses permitted by law.

Stamp of the nursing home and
Dr. Mastragostino's signature.

Stamp: this certifies that the signature of
Dr. Alberto Mastragostino filed at this
Health Board is true and genuine.

Stamp: February 4, 1944
Special Commissioner Dr. Guido Nanni

Seal of the Municipality of Rimini – Health Board.

Viserbella, 6 Febbraio 44

Caro Dottore!

Ieri nel consegnare a Amati la nostra lettera ho dimenticato di allegare il certificat medico per la richiesta del trasferimento nell' Ospedale di San Marino, che mi pregio di inviar-Vi ora, affinché possiate consegnarlo al Comm. Cima.

Di nuovo molti ringraziamenti e cordiali saluti.

A letter of communication related to the certificate.
– State Archive, RSM, Ezio Balducci archive. –

Viserbella, February 6, 1944

Dear Doctor,

Yesterday, when I delivered your letter to Mr. Amati, I overlooked attaching the health certificate to my transfer application to the hospital in San Marino. Please find it enclosed so that you can forward it to Commander Cima.

Many thanks. Yours faithfully,

(Wetzlar)

THE WINTER OF 1944

While Camillo Castiglioni was recovering from a serious case of pneumonia[107] at the convent, young Edoardo Brambilla began to rebel against the usual plate of tripe that his grandmother continued to serve him. Ezio Balducci went on looking for a way to move Hans Wetzlar to San Marino. His wife and daughter had already been renting a room at Mrs. Pignatta's house in the town center. That woman was presumably Sofia Marchi, Erminia Levi Marchi's daughter.[108] Wetzlar himself, instead, was still being guarded at the Villa Salus nursing home. On February 6, he sent another letter to Balducci through their mutual friend Amadori, the pharmacist in Borgo Maggiore. The following day, he sent a medical certificate signed by Dr. Alberto Mastragostino using the same courier: the doctor wrote that the patient had to be transferred to a "*hilly area.*"

During the morning of that Sunday, February 6, 1944, the Black Brigades, which might have been used to give credibility to the "Fascist Republican" farce, became far too credible. Two of them

107. From the letter by Camillo Castiglioni to Alvaro Casali dated November 6, 1952 (Aroldo Casali's collection, RSM).

108. Ezio Balducci archive, letter by Hans and Graziella Wetzlar dated February 6, 1944 (San Marino State Archives, RSM).

went to Borgo Maggiore with weapons in hand; one immediately began to scuffle with Gasperoni. Then after seeing Alvaro Casali walking down the street, he chased after him, firing shots at him. Casali did not have time to take refuge in his house because right in front of the main door a bullet struck him under his arm. They continued shooting in the streets and it seems that Teodoro Lonfernini's wife was grazed by a bullet as well. It was said that the two were stopped while one of them was trying to tear off the tab of a hand grenade.[109]

The bullet that wounded Casali luckily stopped two inches away from his heart. An air pocket prevented a hemorrhage; the dentist's life was saved, although the bullet remained inside his body until the end of his days.[110]

The session of Parliament for the election of the new Captains Regent, whose appointment would start the following April 1, was set for mid-March. In the meantime, rumors circulated that the Fascists were planning further disorders to regain power by force. That day, the Public Palace was guarded, both inside and out, by a large number of gendarmes and guards.

Many members of Parliament had weapons concealed in their pockets. But that was a dramatic turn of events.[111] Nothing happened. Giuliano Gozi took the floor and delivered a powerful speech on the importance of unity in such challenging times.

He also apologized for the serious incident involving Casali and totally dissociated himself from those who had carried out that horrible act. The Fascist leader of San Marino, who had shortly before distanced himself from his colleagues in Rimini by saying that the Republican Fascist Party in San Marino only served to keep the

---

109. Gildo Gasperoni – *Itinerario Politico: a San Marino e in Europa in difesa della democrazia* (Political itinerary: in San Marino and Europe in defense of democracy) – A.I.EP. Editrice, 1983, RSM.

110. From the interview with Aroldo Casali, RSM.

111. Gildo Gasperoni – *Itinerario Politico: a San Marino e in Europa in difesa della democrazia* (Political itinerary: in San Marino and Europe in defense of democracy) – A.I.EP. Editrice, 1983, RSM.

Italian Fascists out of the country, was now ditching those in San Marino as well.

Another very strange but fortunate episode also occurred. Although two out of the three designated pairs to become Captain Regent were formed by at least one member of the Fascist Party, to everyone's amazement, two well-known anti-Fascists were nominated instead. The new heads of state were the surveyor Sanzio Valentini and Professor Francesco Balsimelli.

However, it should be noted that the atmosphere in the homes where many displaced people had taken refuge remained quite peaceful. Of course, they were crammed together and a little hungry as well, but the political tension was not felt much. All they needed to blow things up were disorders among the population. The number of displaced people continued to grow dramatically. Alberto Marvelli went on escorting entire groups of people: he left some of them in the tunnels while others were taken to Father Cesari's, who had finally closed the boarding school and turned it into a huge shelter.

During those days in mid-March, Paolo Tacchi was seriously wounded during an ambush in Cagli. He had to stay put for some time, but his henchmen did not allow themselves a moment's rest.[112]

On March 28, 1944, a very unpleasant episode occurred in Dogana: a naive gendarme, convinced by the Fascist Republicans of Rimini, went over to the house where a man named Giuseppe Babbi was staying. Babbi was a Democrat and a member of the local anti-Fascist forces. The soldier carted him away to the station, where Tacchi's men were waiting for him. They brought Babbi to Rimini and then immediately to the SS command in Bologna, where he was supposed to be shot to death. However, the gendarme had made a serious error: he had created a very dangerous precedent, which the politicians of San Marino had to deal with diplomatically to the point of exhaustion. Even Gumpert, who had managed to establish a di-

112. Antonio Montanari, quoted work.

A detail from the following photograph.

rect communication channel with Ezio Balducci in the meantime, was involved in this situation. Considering his exclusive activity, his colleagues at the German Embassy in Fasano nicknamed him "Saint Marino."[113] In the end, they made it. Their enormous efforts were rewarded, and the Germans recognized that Babbi had been arrested illegally on neutral territory. For this reason, he was not executed.

On April 1, the usual ceremony of investiture of the Captains Regent took place in a cheerful atmosphere. It was photographed just like every typical picture taken of the Heads of State making their first appearance at the entrance of the Public Palace. Photographers still love to take those kinds of pictures today. In that photograph however, something unusual can be noted: Edoardo Brambilla, his

The ceremony of investiture of the Captains Regent on April 1, 1944.
In the background are Anna Pinkert, holding Edoardo Brambilla Grymberg's hand, and Regina Grymberg Brambilla wearing a pair of sunglasses. At the bottom, are some dedicatory words by the Captain Regent Francesco Balsimelli
— CDEC Milan; Courtesy of Edoardo Brambilla Grymberg. —

113. From the interview with Amedeo Montemaggi, Rimini.

grandmother Anna Pinkert, and Regina Grymberg Brambilla, the latter with her face partially covered by sunglasses, were photographed with smiles on their faces while leaning against a column of the Palace as if they wanted to break into that parade of authorities. There is no better way to prove that Jews were living peacefully in San Marino.

To get an idea of how different the atmosphere was in San Marino, it can be said that exactly one week before that event, Colonel Kappler had ordered the execution of 335 men in Rome, in what is remembered as the "Fosse Ardeatine massacre". There were 75 Jews among the victims. Or should you want to try to comprehend what was happening to the Jews during those same hours in the countries occupied by Nazi Germany, well, this can be only guessed at by summing up the extermination, labor, prison, and transit camps to the sub-camps, concentration camps, and collection points. You would count 15,000 structures at work.[114]

While all the hospitalized patients, including Hans Wetzlar, were being transferred from the hospital in Rimini to the one in San Marino, on April 30, the Mayor of Rimini, Ugo Ughi, ordered by the Wehrmacht coastal command, announced that the entire civilian population, within a distance of ten kilometers from the coast, had to be evacuated. This had to be completed by May 15.

The Prefect of Forlì had prepared a plan to forge ahead with the evacuation to "Tebano" in the province of Ravenna. To reach this final destination, they had to walk 114 km in 6 days. In a memo dated April 13, 1944, the Prefect noted that each person could only take some clothing and strictly personal items with them. He reserved the right to negotiate with the German authorities for farmers to have access to their crops and livestock. However, the mass opposition of the population not yet evacuated led the Germans to cease this forced deportation.

The final onslaught against the Gustav Line began on the evening of May 11. A week later, the Poles of the VIII British Army

---

114. Lucy S. Dawidowicz – The war against the Jews 1938-1945, NY Bantam, 1986.

stormed Montecassino. A few days after that, the Allied Army entered Rome. The Germans now faced far more serious problems than those caused by the civilian population of the Emilia Romagna coastal region.[115]

As Ezio Balducci had to go to Milan, he also acted as a courier to collect Regina Grymberg Brambilla's mail. Thanks to this clever

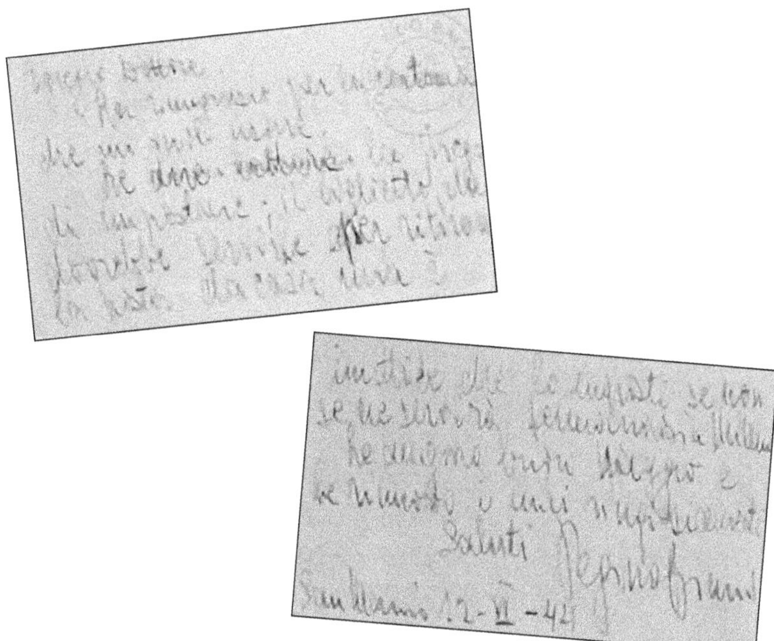

"Dear Doctor, thank you for your kindness. Here are two letters I kindly ask you to mail for me. It will be useless to post the note to collect the mail at my house if you don't use it in Milan. Have a good trip, and I express all my gratitude once again. Best regards - Regina Brambilla - San Marino, VI-12-1944."

A note sent from Regina Grymberg Brambilla to Ezio Balducci on June 12, 1944.
— Courtesy of the State Archives of the Republic of San Marino; Ezio Balducci Archive. —

---

115. Antonio Montanari, quoted work.

"Horse" troops of the Border Militia.
— Courtesy of Giorgio Zani's collection. —

strategy, she managed to avoid having her letters opened by censorship agents and revealing her whereabouts.

The construction of the Gothic Line had finally concluded. It was renamed the "Green Line" and started in Pesaro, on the Adriatic Sea, arriving in Massa Carrara, on the Tyrrhenian Sea, creating a continuous length of 320 km of defensive towers and cannons, hundreds of reinforced concrete shelters, caves carved into the rocks, anti-tank ditches, and minefields. It was equipped with 2,376 machine gun posts, 479 anti-tank guns, numerous mortars, and an unspecified number of assault guns. Naturally, the Germans did not skimp on barbed wire fencing, which stretched along the line for no less than 1,200 km.[116] Further south, the Gustav Line had been completely destroyed. This led everyone to anticipate that the worst was yet to come. The hard-fought war was inexorably drawing closer to San Marino, even as everyone anxiously awaited its liberation by the Allies.

There were nearly 70,000 displaced people. Along with the high number of refugees, other issues arose due to incursions from the Fascists of Rimini, who did not always visit San Marino for pleasure, combined with the harsh stance of the German Army. As a result, the Government decided to establish a Border Militia, prompting the issuance of an enrollment notice. The minimum requirement for admission was a high school diploma, or ideally, a college degree. "*We had no weapon besides dialogue and diplomacy to counter potential problems,*"[117] said Giorgio Zani. Colonel Alvaro Casali was chosen to oversee the operation; Federico Bigi was appointed Captain while Giorgio Zani, the only one with some military training, was assigned the rank of First Lieutenant. There were also two Second Lieutenants, Gaetano Belloni and Virginio Reffi, the latter being particularly significant since he spoke some German. He had studied it with the aim of impressing Edith, the most beautiful blonde woman in San

116. Mimmo Franzinelli, *RSI – La Repubblica del Duce 1943-1945* (RSI – the Duce's Republic 1943-1945), Mondadori, 2007, Milan (pag. 6).

117. From the interview with Attorney Giorgio Zani, RSM.

Marino. About sixty young men enlisted, driven by a strong sense of patriotism and a touch of audacity.

As soon as Paolo Tacchi realized that it would be more challenging for him to carry out his usual raids in San Marino, or better yet, that he would have to obtain permission to enter due to the newly formed Border Militia, he sent Gozi and Balducci an astonishing request. He demanded that the authorities of San Marino complete a public security form for every person present in the territory, granting the Republican Fascist Party in Rimini access to this information whenever necessary. In doing so, San Marino would be recognized as a "Town of the Italian Social Republic."[118] Tacchi completely dis-

The Border Militia General Staff:
Above from the left, Cap. Federico Bigi, Col. Alvaro Casali and 1st Lt. Giorgio Zani;
bottom, from the left 2nd Lt. Gaetano Bellon and 2nd Lt. Virginio Reffi.
— Courtesy of Giorgio Zani's collection. —

118. Ezio Balducci Archive, letter by Major Lutze dated June 24, 1944, State Archives, RSM.

regarded the independence and neutrality of this Sovereign State, which was recognized by the more powerful country of Germany.

While the young volunteers were training to act as soon as possible, a small group of firefighters was also being organized. Hundreds of volunteers across the territory worked diligently to draw large white crosses on the fields near the borders and on the roofs of the houses.

At that point, even the airplanes going to bomb the town of Rimini, which had become nothing more than a pile of rubble by then, could clearly recognize the Republic of San Marino while flying over the area at a high altitude.

Everybody's favorite pastime in San Marino was to crowd along the ridge of Mount Titano and watch the massacre take place along the coast. Some children even had binoculars. The German soldiers had traded them for a few bottles of wine, which the children had secretly stolen from the cellars of their houses.[119]

Borgo Maggiore seen from above with the white crosses on the roofs in June 1944.
— Photo by MW, Republic of San Marino. —

119. From the interview with Gian Piero Gozi, RSM.

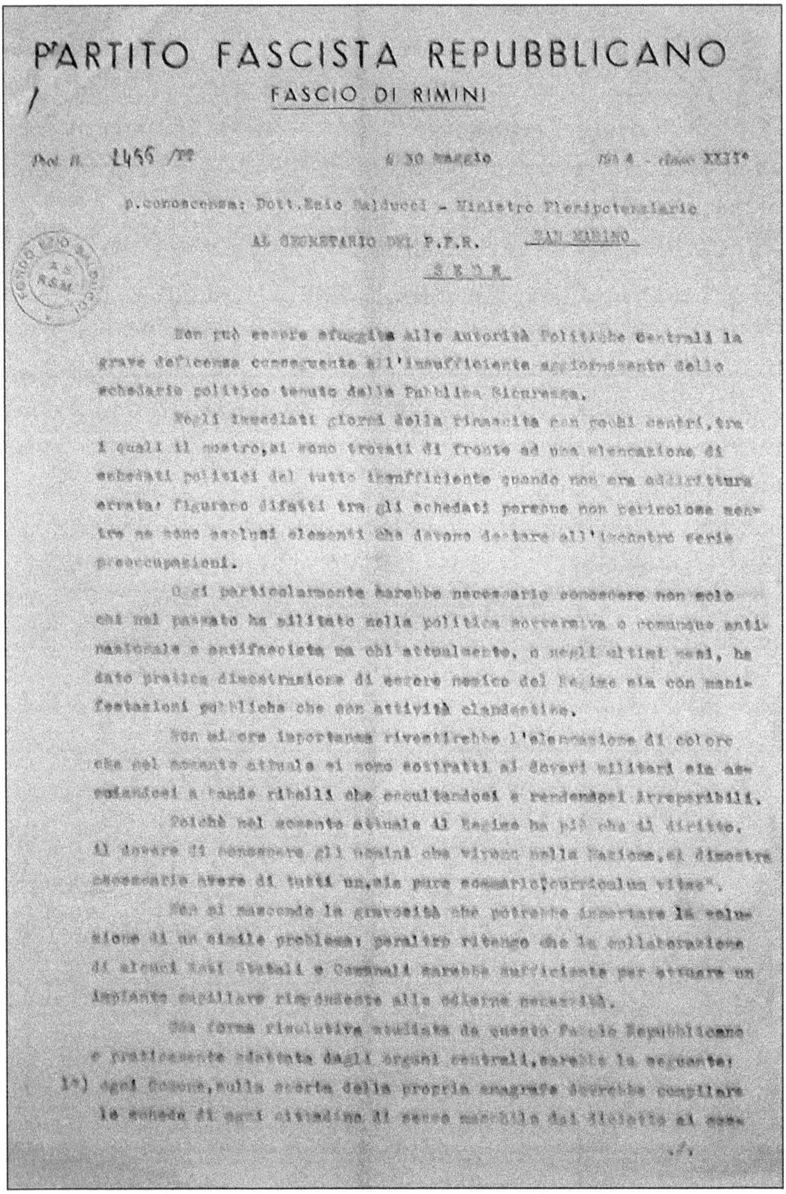

PARTITO FASCISTA REPUBBLICANO
FASCIO DI RIMINI

Prot. N. 1456 /PF — lì 30 maggio 1944 - Anno XXII°

p.conoscenza: Dott.Ezio Balducci - Ministro Plenipotenziario

AL SEGRETARIO DEL P.F.R. SAN MARINO
SEDE

Non può essere sfuggita alle Autorità Politiche Centrali la grave deficenza conseguente all'insufficiente aggiornamento dello schedario politico tenuto dalla Pubblica Sicurezza.

Negli immediati giorni della rinascita non pochi centri, tra i quali il nostro, si sono trovati di fronte ad una elencazione di schedati politici del tutto insufficiente quando non era addirittura errata: figurano difatti tra gli schedati persone non pericolose mentre ne sono esclusi elementi che devono destare all'incontro serie preoccupazioni.

Oggi particolarmente sarebbe necessario conoscere non solo chi nel passato ha militato nella politica sovversiva o comunque antinazionale e antifascista ma chi attualmente, o negli ultimi mesi, ha dato pratica dimostrazione di essere nemico del Regime sia con manifestazioni pubbliche che con attività clandestine.

Non minore importanza rivestirebbe l'elencazione di coloro che nel momento attuale si sono sottratti ai doveri militari sia associandosi a bande ribelli che occultandosi e rendendosi irreperibili.

Poichè nel momento attuale il Regime ha più che il diritto, il dovere di conoscere gli uomini che vivono nella Nazione, si dimostra necessario avere di tutti un, sia pure sommario "curriculum vitae".

Non si nasconde la gravosità che potrebbe importare la soluzione di un simile problema: peraltro ritengo che la collaborazione di alcuni Enti Statali e Comunali sarebbe sufficiente per attuare un impianto capillare rispondente alle odierne necessità.

Una forma risolutiva studiata da questo Fascio Repubblicano e praticamente sistemata dagli organi centrali, sarebbe la seguente:
1°) ogni Comune, sulla scorta della propria anagrafe dovrebbe compilare le schede di ogni cittadino di sesso maschile dai diciotto ai sess./.

First page of a letter sent by Paolo Tacchi on May 30, 1944
— Courtesy of the State Archives of the Republic of San Marino. —

REPUBLICAN FASCIST PARTY
FASCIO OF RIMINI

Protocol # 2455/IT May 30, 1944, year XXII

c.c. Dr. Ezio Balducci – Minister Plenipotentiary

To the Secretary of the SAN MARINO R.F.P.

AT HIS HEADQUARTERS

The serious deficiency resulting from the insufficient update of the political files kept by the Public Security Office cannot have gone unnoticed by the central political authority.

In the first days of rebirth, various offices, among which is ours as well, had to cope with a totally meager list of people filed for political reasons. In some cases, these lists were even incorrect, as they included people who posed no danger, while other individuals worth worrying about were excluded.

Now, it would be particularly necessary to know who not only subversive, anti-national, or anti-Fascist individuals were in the past but also those who, in the last few months, have proven to be enemies of the regime either through clandestine activities or public demonstrations.

It would also be equally important to compile a list of those who are not currently complying with their military obligations, either by joining rebel groups or evading detection.

As in these days, the regime has not only the right but the duty to know the people who live within the territory of the nation; it is essential to have a short résumé of each citizen.

I do not want to minimize the efforts that may be required to solve this problem; however, I think that suitable collaboration between some State and Local bodies might be enough to establish a comprehensive network that can meet today's needs.

The following would be a final format designed by this Republican Fascist Section and adapted by central bodies:

1°) Starting from local Registry Offices, each municipality should fill in a form for every male citizen aged between 18 and 60,

RTITO FASCISTA REPUBBLICANO

FASCIO DI RIMINI

Prot. N. li 194 - Anno

- 2 -

santa anni limitandosi peraltro alle sole notizie anagrafiche (cognome, nome, paternità, maternità, data di nascita, stato civile, residenza) ;

2°) le schede così compilate dai comuni dovrebbero essere passate ad un organo politico o di polizia per l'annotazione di tutte le altre indicazioni di carattere politico, giudiziario, penale, militare.

E' indifferente che tale schedario debba essere affidato al Partito o alla Polizia Repubblicana; ove si ritenesse opportuno affidarlo a quest'ultima i Fasci potranno essere autorizzati ad estrarne una copia per il loro uso interno.

Molte sono le fonti alle quali le Autorità Politiche e di Polizia potranno far capo per ottenere le indicazioni necessarie alla compilazione di ogni singola scheda; certamente più di tutte le altre sarà efficace la collaborazione dei singoli Fasci che in questi ultimi mesi hanno avuto la possibilità di conoscere l'attività dei singoli nei confronti della Politica Nazionale.

La proposta che questo Fascio Repubblicano avanza con la presente non vuole essere risolutiva di un problema che ha moltiformi aspetti e che a seconda delle località può dimostrarsi di maggiore o minore necessità; è peraltro pacifico che si renda opportuno una migliore attrezzatura dell'attuale sistema informativo politico dal momento che è proprio oggi in cui si sono rivelati i veri sentimenti di tutti i cittadini italiani e solo oggi, con maggiore tranquillità, è possibile prendere nota dei sentimenti stessi per averli presenti in un domani in cui, l'immancabile rinascita della Nazione Italiana consiglierà la massa a virare ancora una volta verso il Regime e verso lo stato Fascista.

Mi permetto allegare un modello della scheda che questo Fascio ha studiato ben lieto se le superiori gerarchie vorranno prendere in considerazione la proposta che con la presente avanzo.

IL SEGRETARIO DEL FASCIO REPUBBLICANO
(Paolo Tacchi)

Back page of a letter sent by Paolo Tacchi on May 30, 1944.
— Courtesy of the State Archives of the Republic of San Marino. —

including only their personal data (last name, first name, father and mother's names, date of birth, marital status, and place of residence).

2°) The forms filled in by each municipality should be sent to a political or police body for the recording of any other political, legal, criminal, or military information.

It is not important whether these files are entrusted to the Party or the Republican Police. Should it be deemed to be more suitable to have them kept by the latter, the Fascist Sections will be allowed to make copies of the forms for their own use.

Political and Police Authorities can refer to various sources to obtain the necessary information to complete the forms. The collaboration between the various Fascist Sections will be the most efficient means as the latter have had the possibility to know the activities of every single citizen towards National politics in the last few months.

The project proposed by this Republican Fascist Section does not want to be the final solution to such a multi-sided problem. Actually, for each Section, there could be various aspects to deal with, while it is absolutely evident that the present political information system needs improvement. These days, in fact, the true feelings of all Italian citizens have become clear, so it is now possible to document these attitudes with more serenity, to preserve them for the future when the inevitable rebirth of the Italian Nation will cause the masses to turn once again towards the Fascist Regime and State.

Please find herewith enclosed a draft form drawn up by this Fascist Section. I will be grateful if your highest authorities can take this proposal into consideration.

The Secretary of the Republican Fascist Section
(Paolo Tacchi)

State Border, the German soldiers had the signs in English removed.
— Courtesy of the State Archives of the Republic of San Marino. —

Picture of the Border Militia swearing-in on June 25, 1944.
— Courtesy of Giorgio Zani's collection. —

On June 24, Major Lutze, in charge of the coastal area of Rimini, distributed signs written in German to be placed along the entire border. They read: "Soldiers are not allowed to enter the neutral territory of the Republic of San Marino". He also had the words written in English removed from the signs placed at the borders. They might have considered them to be an omen of bad luck, or perhaps offensive to Nazi Germany.[120]

On June 25, everything was ready at the Public Palace. At 5 p.m., the troops of the "Border Militia" arrived. In the Council Hall, General Onofrio Fattori took oath by reading the formula from the book of "military discipline" dated May 27, 1872 in the presence of the Captains Regent, Sanzio Balsimelli and Francesco Valentini: *"I swear to guard my homeland, its independence, its freedom; to defend its Constitutions, the integrity of its territory and its legitimate sovereign Parliament, the General Council of the Sixties, with the Captains Regent, who represent it. I swear to pay them immediate and perfect obedience, to ensure compliance with the laws, to give my contribution to the maintenance of public order and public peace, to guarantee the life and goods of each individual."*[121]

120. Ezio Balducci archive, letter by Major Lutze dated May 30, 1944, State Archives, RSM.

121. State Archives, RSM.

JUNE 26, 1944

On the morning of June 26, 1944, the sixty-three soldiers received their orders from the command, which was temporarily housed at Palazzo Begni at the time. Their first task was to "facilitate the entry of refugees"; their second one was to "safely prevent the entry of armed soldiers."

Meanwhile, Amedeo Montemaggi was in San Giovanni in Galilea, a small town on the edge of the Valmarecchia valley, about ten kilometers from San Marino via a direct route. On October 29, he had been fired by the newspaper Il Resto del Carlino for disclosing Mussolini's love affair, in which he forced Claretta Petacci to have an abortion after she became pregnant during one of his numerous romantic escapades in the Emilia-Romagna region.

Well, on that sunny morning, Montemaggi stood on the promontory of the village where he had lived since leaving the tormented town of Rimini. From that spot, he could overlook the entire Riviera. He saw a flock of Allied bombers from the "Desert Air Force" approaching. At first, he thought it was the usual torment of the coastal town. He was astonished, however, when he realized that those planes were dropping their bombs on San Marino: *"It seemed impossible; I knew that San Marino was bursting at the seams with refugees. I could not believe my eyes. They were violating the neutrality of that small country right in front of my eyes. I felt helpless!"*[122]

---

122. From the interview with Amedeo Montemaggi, Rimini.

At 11:31 am, the explosions began and continued rapidly, one after the other. They struck the old town center, the heart of the country. The first explosion occurred near the Cliff Gateway, close to the Convent of Saint Clare. At that time, the nuns were housing 65 young girls, most of whom had been entrusted to them by displaced people. They were all in the courtyard, waiting for lunch to be served. Everyone ran for their lives. The only one left in the middle of the garden was an old nun, looking up at the sky in speechless wonder. One of the Sisters saw her from inside and went out to get her. As she dragged the nun inside, she asked, *"What are you doing out there?"* The other replied, *"I saw Saint Marinus. He was enormous, and he was protecting our convent from the bombs with his arms."*

"Don't tell anyone or they'll think you're out of your mind," said the other.[123]

The blasts were terrible. Renzo Bonelli had witnessed other bombings when he lived in Rimini, but the sound of the bombs there was muted and deep. *"Up here instead, on the rock of this mountain, it was deafening due to the echo of the surrounding valleys. During the first explosion, I thought a plane had crashed; only later did I realize that it was a "bombing."*[124]

On the road leading to the Country Gateway, the people running to find shelter fell to the ground one right after the other. They were mowed down by a myriad of splinters and stones. These powerful bullets ricocheted off the ground in every direction. The Bellavista hotel was struck directly, and a bomb exploded just a few meters from the school filled with children.

Carla Nicolini, along with her mother, began to run from their home to a shelter near the cliff. They met Alvaro Casali, who, heedless of the fact that a few months earlier he had been wounded by a bullet that had stopped two inches from his heart, was running up from Borgo Maggiore and shouting that the Public Palace had been

123. Statement by the nuns at the Monastery of Saint Clare, RSM.

124. From the interview with Renzo Bonelli, RSM.

bombed. Carla, who was young at the time, started to give up all hope after hearing the news. Even worse, she then remembered that her father was at a meeting of the Financial Committee right inside the building. She began to run toward the center of town. Along the way, she could see a horrifying sight of mangled bodies lying everywhere. She immediately feared that her father was among those corpses as well: *"So as I was going up to the old town, every time I ran into a corpse lying face down, I would turn it upside down to see if it was my father."*[125] Then, Carla finally saw her father. He, too, was running down to see how his family was.

Giuseppina Tamagnini, while running home, had to step aside to let two small German open-top military cars pass by. *"They were blowing their horns to make people move off the street. They had been on a visit to the Public Palace. In one of those cars, I saw an officer whose chest was full of decorations. He was covering his ear with his hand, and a visible trail of blood was running down his arm. Soon after, I met my brother Giorgio. He was more concerned about the fact that he had lost his beret while he was running away than about the bombs. We had to go and look for it before fleeing."*[126]

Renzo Bonelli ran towards the school with his mother to find out what had happened to his little sister, but when they reached the street leading to the school, they encountered an impenetrable wall of dust. They stopped in their tracks, fearing that the building had collapsed completely. Then suddenly, they spotted little Maria Antonietta emerging from the dense cloud with her schoolbag on her shoulders, completely covered in sand and with two long trails of tears running down her face.[127]

Giorgio Zani requested permission to leave the command of the Border Militia to go home and check on his family's conditions. Heedless of all the rubble blocking the streets, he climbed over every-

---

125. From the interview with Carla Nicolini, RSM.

126. From the interview with Giuseppina Tamagnini, RSM.

127. From the interview with Renzo Bonelli, RSM.

thing and reached his house in a few moments. When his mother saw him completely covered in dust, she fainted from the emotions and tumbled down the stairs, injuring herself quite seriously.[128]

Maria José Mandelli had, in the meantime, run towards her mother, who was desperately shouting on the street: "My children, where are my children?". Vittoria and Ruggero were inside the school while her baby Patrizia Marina was in her stroller, which the nanny had let go of and was rolling down the street out of control near their house.[129]

Inside the school, Gian Piero Gozi was looking at his friends, who were trying to pick up their teacher, Mrs. Otilia, off the floor. The blast had caused her to fall, but since she was rather obese, only the janitor was able to move her. Gian Piero saw his brother Gemino run into the building. Gemino, who was much older than him, had a son in the same school. "*Have you seen Manlio?*" he asked. "*Manlio has already fled towards the train tunnel,*" I replied. "*Then he grabbed my arm and quickly dragged me to the tunnel as well. Just outside the Country Gateway, I saw all the dead bodies lying on the road. On the right, I recognized Bruno Reffi, there, on the ground. I had seen him the night before at the Titano Theatre, and now they were covering him with a sheet.*"[130]

Almost everyone was running towards the train tunnel. Giuseppina Tamagnini and her family first entered the woods below the Third Tower. Carla Nicolini set off for Cà Berlone with her family. Her father had bought a donkey with a small cart from a passing farmer: "He used it to transport my grandmother, who was very ill." They walked briskly, but exactly thirty minutes later, a second squadron of bombers flew by. This time, the bomb clusters fell on Santa Mustiola, west of the town center, directly on the road that Nicolini and his family were using to escape from the hell they had just left.

128. From the interview with Attorney Giorgio Zani, RSM.

129. From the interview with Maria José Mandelli, Reggio Calabria.

130. From the interview with Gian Piero Gozi, RSM.

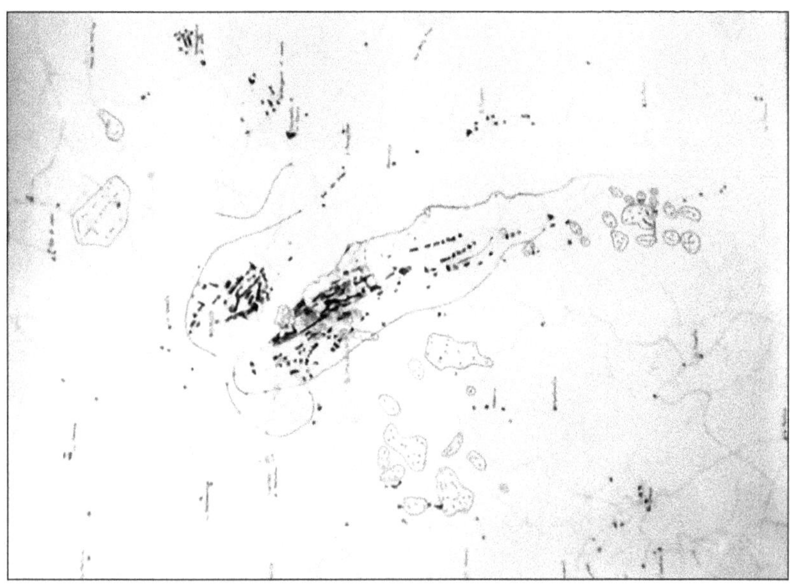

Topographic reconstruction of the points where the bombs exploded.
— Courtesy of Giorgio Zani's collection. —

"During the first explosions, we all threw ourselves into the ditch at the side of the road. We remained lying there while we heard loud blasts and shrapnel whizzing over our heads. As soon as everything was over, we realized that none of us had thought about our grandma, so we ran out to the road to see where she was. She was down the street, still on the cart being pulled by the donkey. The poor woman hadn't noticed a thing because, besides being very sick, she was also completely deaf."[131]

Giuseppina Tamagnini watched that bombing and all the other ones from the top of the Third Tower.[132] There were six altogether, and the last one took place at 2 p.m. on the dot. The young soldiers were immediately sent out to assist and transport, by every means possible, over 200 injured people on the roads and in the homes hit by the 243 British bombs. Sixty-three people died: forty were from San Marino, while twenty-three were refugees. Franco Lo Monaco was

131. From the interview with Carla Nicolini, RSM.

132. From the interview with Giuseppina Tamagnini, RSM.

Valloni House, in the heart of the old town center, was partially destroyed by the bombs.
– Courtesy of Giorgio Zani's collection. –

among the wounded. He had been struck by numerous shrapnel near the house where he lived with his wife.[133]

Ezio Balducci relied on Romano Michelotti's reckless driving. He had already tempted fate several times on his motorcycle while delivering letters to all the commands of northern Italy. It is said that he preferred traveling during air raid warnings because the streets were free from traffic at those times. The two men made their way to Fasano del Garda, where they arrived late at night. Gumpert immediately organized a meeting between Balducci and the Ambassador, Rudolf Rahn, who offered him money after learning about the grave incident. However, Balducci, out of pride, refused his generous gesture. He instead asked for medicine, coal, and a squad of experts to defuse the unexploded bombs.[134]

In San Marino, everybody had found shelter in the railway tunnels before sundown: the citizens, refugees, and Jews; they were all sharing the darkness and dampness of the rocks of Mount Titano. Gian Piero Gozi recalled that when he arrived in the tunnel, he found himself face to face with a braying donkey: "The bombing had caught a farmer by surprise nearby, so he sought refuge in there along with that frightened animal."[135]

The blue and white train was promptly positioned at the end of the first tunnel and utilized as a hospital. After a while, Maria José Mandelli finally found her grandfather, Leopold: "*He was in a bathrobe and slippers; he was having a shower when the bombing started and ran out of his house dressed like that.*"[136]

The Captains Regent immediately wrote a letter to the German command. They begged them to prevent their soldiers from entering the territory of San Marino, either in groups or individually, to avoid

---

133. Registry Office of the Republic of San Marino, death certificate, file no. 102 dated June 30, 1944.

134. From the interview with Amedeo Montemaggi, Rimini.

135. From the interview with Gian Piero Gozi, RSM.

136. From the interview with Maria José Mandelli, Reggio Calabria.

Another view of the Valloni House.
— Courtesy of Giorgio Zani's collection. —

reprisals from the Allies. The Vatican, which was also promptly informed of the incident, sent a letter of protest to England.[137]

At the command of the Border Militia, Virginio Reffi was entrusted with the challenging task of secretly crossing the Gothic Line and reaching the Allies.[138] The idea was to establish direct contact with the attackers and inform them about the actual situation in San Marino. Reffi successfully carried out the tasks. He reached the front line, where he met the first battalions near the town of Urbino. Then he moved on to Pescara, arriving four days later. The bombers that had caused the massacre had taken off from that town. Meanwhile, three days of mourning were declared in San Marino.

There was an uprising at the bakery; the workers were afraid to stay and work there while all the others were safe inside the tunnels.

Giorgio Zani, sitting next to his mother, who is knitting outside the train tunnel.
– Courtesy of Giorgio Zani's collection. –

137. Verter Casali, *Appunti di Storia* (History notes) in *Il Corriere Sammarinese*, Issue no. 45, Friday, May 14, 2004.

138. From the interview with Attorney Giorgio Zani, RSM.

Displaced people next to the main station tunnel.
— Courtesy of Giorgio Zani's collection. —

Count Manzoni's "living room" in the tunnel.
The Count is in the middle, while on his left is Giorgio Zani.
— Courtesy of Giorgio Zani's collection. —

Life in the tunnels in the summer of 1944.
— Courtesy of Giorgio Zani's collection. —

Other moments of life in the tunnels.
— Courtesy of Giorgio Zani's collection. —

Other moments of life in the tunnels.
— Courtesy of Giorgio Zani's collection. —

As a result, three young soldiers from the Border Militia were called to guard the building. They were tasked with sounding the alarm should any other planes arrive. Giordano Reffi was among them: *"They left us there without any food or water. During the third night, a baker named Silvestro Rossi came out. He saw we were starving, so he got some knives and went over to the other side of the street where a donkey was lying dead because of the bombings. He cut off its leg and cooked it for us in the oven along with the bread.... It was delicious."*[139]

At the same time, a new community life was forming in the tunnels. There were no social distinctions; everyone could see what the others were doing, and the news traveled by word of mouth as if on a telegraph wire. Giuseppina Tamagnini, who was in the first portion of the tunnel close to the station, knew that two Jewish families had been living at the end of the same tunnel for a long time, but they told her not to tell anyone.

"There was a German soldier who occasionally appeared at the entrance of the tunnel and asked questions. He would inquire if there were

139. From the interview with Giordano Reffi, RSM.

Some displaced people also occupied the covered areas of the cemetery of Montalbo.
— Courtesy of Giorgio Zani's collection. —

people who spoke with a foreign accent. A language teacher camping right in front of me often did. She pretended not to speak any language except Italian, but I was present when she gave English lessons to two girls from Bologna. One was a Mandelli."[140]

Maria José Mandelli added: *"She wasn't a real teacher. She was a hairdresser, a friend of my mother's. She had worked in Paris and wanted my cousin and me to have some French lessons. What an incredible experience that tunnel was! My grandfather Leopold slept in a wheelbarrow; my cousin and I had learned to shower with a bottle of water each. We used to go to the middle of the tunnel where there was a hole facing the cliff. A wooden platform, suspended in mid-air, had been built overlooking the precipice. We would take turns covering each other up with a cloth in order to wash ourselves!"*[141]

Every morning, Otto Ruhl would leave the tunnel with a small folding table. He set it up in front of the entrance and prepared some cigarettes, rolling them one by one. Celio Gozi recalled in his memoir: "He always had some excellent smuggled tobacco and never failed to offer me a cigarette."[142]

Renzo Bonelli remembered him as a nice old man: *"Mr. Ruhl used to pass by holding that table under his arm and tell us kids with his German accent: watch the legs, watch the legs. It is not that he actually wanted to hit anyone with that object; he just wanted to be funny!"*[143]

Giorgio Zani only went to the tunnel in the evening to visit his family: *"Count Bartolomeo Manzoni had built his private living room with some cardboard and a wooden case. We used to spend pleasant evenings together."*[144]

---

140. From the interview with Giuseppina Tamagnini, RSM.

141. From the interview with Maria José Mandelli, Reggio Calabria.

142. Celio Gozi, *Memoria sugli Ebrei a San Marino durante l'ultimo conflitto.* (Memorial about the Jews in San Marino during the recent conflict) – Gozi's Collection, RSM.

143. From the interview with Renzo Bonelli, RSM.

144. From the interview with Attorney Giorgio Zani, RSM.

The fields and the woods were full of displaced people.
— Courtesy of Giorgio Zani's collection. —

A woman preparing a "piadina" on a wooden box.
— Courtesy of Giorgio Zani's collection. —

Some displaced people traveling to San Marino.
— Courtesy of Giorgio Zani's collection. —

Columns of displaced people walking to San Marino in the area of Faetano.
— Courtesy of Giorgio Zani's collection. —

Other displaced people guided by a priest heading to San Marino.
— Courtesy of Giorgio Zani's collection. —

Edoardo Brambilla recalled that occasionally, he would run along the tracks, shouting that a bomb was coming. He enjoyed creating a bit of panic.[145]

Giuseppina Tamagnini reminisced when her brother Roberto, who at the time was two years old, caught pneumonia: *"My mom went back home with him. Otherwise, he wouldn't recover in that place. We, instead, remained in the tunnel. She would occasionally come to visit and bring us some food. I remember that one day she brought some handmade pasta with sauce and roasted rabbit with potatoes. It was the most delicious lunch I had ever eaten. Then one day Mandelli and Michelotti went to the cake factory and made a large quantity of miniature cakes. Mandelli himself brought them to the tunnel and gave them out to all of us, one each."*[146]

Gian Piero Gozi only stayed in the tunnel for three days: "My grandmother had a big room in her house which was half carved into the rock, so she put mattresses on the floor, and we all settled in there."[147]

Not everyone went to the tunnels. Marino Muccioli did not even spend a single day there. Along with a young surveyor, he accepted the job to dig small air-raid shelters around the country. The first one was to be built in a wall of rock near the hospital. The surveyor reassured Muccioli that he was an expert and asked him to chip away, with a chisel, a series of holes where he would then place some sticks of dynamite. "Are you sure of what you're doing?" he asked the surveyor. "Trust me," replied the other. The explosion blew off the roof of the Convent of Saint Francis and broke the last windowpanes that had remained intact after the June 26th bombing. This was the reason why the local rulers decided there was no longer any need for air-raid shelters in San Marino.[148]

---

145. From the interview with Giuseppina Tamagnini, RSM.

146. Ibid.

147. From the interview with Gian Piero Gozi, RSM.

148. From the interview with Marino Muccioli, RSM.

Regardless of the bombing, after a few days, the flow of refugees towards the small Republic resumed. Bread was rationed to 50 grams daily per person. Some power lines were down, so the old stone mills were set back into motion to grind wheat. Ezio Balducci once again relied on the reckless motorcyclist Romano Michelotti. On July 12, Balducci and Michelotti raced back to Fasano del Garda, where Balducci asked his old friend Gumpert to help him obtain "a" railroad car of fuel from Germany. Gumpert immediately called the man in charge of supplies, General Layers, and said, "We need to send three railroad cars of fuel to San Marino right now". The officer replied that he did not have three cars available; at most, he could give him two. Gumpert turned and winked at Balducci. Then he said, "I'm sorry, but we can only give you two cars". Balducci played the part and pretended to be disappointed, but when he got home, he wrote a touching thank-you letter to Gumpert.[149]

But there were other problems in addition to those caused by the displaced people and the war, the real one, which had already made its presence known, loudly and clearly, on June 26. There was always Ermenegildo Gasperoni, the former Spanish War soldier who undauntedly continued his fight against fascism along with his companions. This was all part of the idea of democracy and the "pursuit of freedom," as he used to call it, but unfortunately, those subversive actions always attracted the attention of the nasty "Black Brigades." "Gildo" was arrested on May 1 on the accusation of violating the ban on strikes. He escaped on the same day but was recaptured a month later, along with some people from Rimini, during a clandestine meeting near the cemetery of Montalbo.[150] On that occasion, the authorities of San Marino had to struggle hard to keep him in the Republic.

---

149. Ezio Balducci Archive, Letter to Gumpert dated July 22, 1944 (State Archives, RSM).

150. Gildo Gasperoni – *Itinerario Politico: a San Marino e in Europa in difesa della democrazia* (Political itinerary: in San Marino and Europe in defense of democracy) – A.I.EP. Editrice, 1983, RSM.

The Fascists, in the meantime, had dragged those from Rimini to the SS command in Forlì, where a firing squad was waiting for them. Gasperoni was supposed to meet the same fate: the Germans wanted him at all costs. However, Federico Bigi and Ezio Balducci found a way to keep him in San Marino, while the others managed to escape thanks to a fortuitous bombing that occurred just before they were executed.

Another moment of panic ensued in mid-July, when the Fascist leader Paolo Tacchi noticed a bullet hole in the door of his car while leaving Serravalle. Realizing that someone within the territory of San Marino was trying to kill him, he decided to take it out on the entire country.[151] On that same evening, he returned with a large group of Fascist supporters of the Republic of Salò and terrorized the population for several hours until Balducci managed to calm him down. However, Tacchi reflected on the episode, and a few days later, he returned to San Marino. He unexpectedly entered the tunnels, captured seventy-three young men, and took them across the border, accusing them of being draft dodgers. The men were all crowded together in a field in the vicinity of Santa Aquilina, under the supervision of some German soldiers. Giorgio Zani, Giovanni Michelotti, and Virginio Reffi intervened and managed to convince the Germans that the young men were all from San Marino and, for that reason, they could not be arrested. The Germans asked them to prove what they were saying, so a militiaman ran back to San Marino to obtain documents from anyone he could find, then he rushed back to Santa Aquilina to demonstrate that the prisoners were actually citizens of the Republic. In the confusion, the Germans believed the three militiamen and freed all the prisoners. This time, the survivors walked back to their shelters under the watchful eye of the volunteers of the Border Militia and not under the threat of the Nazi-Fascists.[152]

---

151. Antonio Montanari, quoted work.

152. Statement by Giovanni Michelotti, RSM.

Borgo Maggiore, displaced people queuing for the bread.
— Photo by MW, Republic of San Marino. —

But misfortunes, you know, never come alone. No one had noticed that the bombing had caused the inadequate water supply system of San Marino to come into contact with its sewer system. On July 22, Doctor Enea Suzzi Valli informed the Government that he had found some refugees suffering from typhoid fever.[153] The cases multiplied hour after hour, and no appropriate medicine was available at all. Balducci immediately turned to Gumpert, who asked Germany for some. The medicine arrived in San Marino on August 8, when the number of confirmed typhoid cases had risen to over 200, and unfortunately, there were several victims among them.

Carla Nicolini was one of the people who contracted typhus: "I felt really bad; I even lost my hair, and it took several months to get over it completely."

Gerard Richard Gumpert at the State border in Gualdicciolo with some young men of the Border Militia.
— Gothic Line Archives; Courtesy of Amedeo Montemaggi. —

153. Ezio Balducci Archive; Medical report by Dr. Enea Suzzi Valli dated July 22, 1944 (State Archives, RSM).

On July 27, a German officer placed three batteries of cannons within the border of San Marino in the Faetano area. A letter of complaint was sent to Kesselring, who had replaced Rommel at General Command a few months earlier. Giovanni Michelotti saw Gumpert at the location, working hard to have the cannons removed.[154] Three days later, a medical officer arrived and requested that three government buildings be converted into German military hospitals. Additionally, the Government of San Marino was informed that, if needed, the German Army would cross the border, completely disregarding Rommel's promise! Therefore, it was decided to send a mission to Mussolini in Salò and to the German Ambassador in Fasano del Garda.

On August 1, the Captain Regent Francesco Balsimelli, the Secretary of the Republican Fascist Party Giuliano Gozi, the Special Delegate Ezio Balducci, Leonida Suzzi Valli and Marino Belluzzi left for Fasano del Garda.[155]

That same evening, they met Gerard Gumpert, who introduced the delegation to Ambassador Rudolf Rahn. Balducci spoke in French and conveyed the concerns of the people of San Marino regarding Hitler. The following morning, they met Mussolini, and at the end of their discussions, the "Duce" calmed them down by saying: "You will be surrounded by flames, but you won't be burnt!"

On August 12, several people from San Marino fell into a trap set by the Nazi-Fascists. Giuseppe and Armando Renzi, Luigi Giancecchi, Nazzareno Arzilli, and, as usual, Ermenegildo Gasperoni were arrested. Some of them had been given guns to be sent to unidentified anti-Fascists. If these individuals had at least checked those weapons, they would have noticed the deception: none of them had firing pins. Again, Balducci and Bigi had to negotiate to avoid their deportation, that is, their "execution." This time it was much more difficult than before: facing them was Marshal Kurt Schutze of the Gestapo. A few

---

154. Statement by Giovanni Michelotti, RSM.

155. From the report of the Captain Regent Francesco Balsimelli to the Great and General Council dated 09-23-1944, State Archives, RSM.

months prior, Schutze, who was under the command of Herbert Kappler, had organized, along with Erik Pribke, the massacre at the Fosse Ardeatine and, before that, the house-to-house search for Jews in the Roman ghetto.

Giuseppe Renzi saw Balducci crying in despair, that time.[156] It was Renzi himself who inadvertently came up with the idea of how to save everyone. He exclaimed: *"I don't at all want to become the President of San Marino!"* A light bulb went off in Balducci's mind, and thanks to Federico Bigi, who persisted throughout the night until dawn, it bore fruit. The negotiations concluded with the thesis that the people arrested were formulating a plan against the Government of San Marino, not against the Germans or the supporters of the Republic of Salò.[157]

In order to prove this thesis, they even prepared a dossier. Schutze insisted for several days before giving up completely.

In the meantime, life in the tunnels became increasingly difficult. Giuseppe Mandelli took advantage of the fact that the rear part of his house leaned against the rock. He dug out a small shelter and moved his whole family there: *"We entered that cave from the kitchen,"* said Maria José. *"It was very small, so we were all crammed in there. We couldn't move. During the day, we stayed in the house, while at night, we all piled into the cave."*[158]

August 25th could have been the day of the Apocalypse in San Marino. In Rimini, Lieutenant Colonel Christiani, of the 303rd Regiment of the 162nd Turkmen Infantry Division, was prepared to invade and raid San Marino with his 1,500 soldiers.[159]

But these names and numbers do not make sense by themselves. They must be explained to understand the danger San Marino faced that day. "Lieutenant Colonel Christiani" presided over the

---

156. Giuseppe Renzi's statement, RSM.

157. Antonio Montanari, quoted work.

158. From the interview with Maria José Mandelli, Reggio Calabria.

159. From the interview with Amedeo Montemaggi, Rimini.

court-martial that condemned to death the "three martyrs of Rimini" on August 15, 1944. The 303rd Regiment was formed by infantry assault troops united with the "Panzer-Division," while the 162nd Division, established in 1942, consisted of "Turkmen" troops, also known as "Mongols" and nicknamed "Hitler's dogs" because of their ferocity. They had joined the feared SS and were commanded by General Ralph von Heygendorff. It should be noted that the 162nd Division had been personally commissioned and established by Himmler, the creator of the extermination camps.

When Secretary of State Babboni was informed about the upcoming raid, he immediately sent Balducci to the Coastal Command, where soldiers, with weapons on their shoulders, were already prepared to move. Although he initially did not want to participate, Tacchi became involved in the mission as well. Balducci revived his memories and reminded him of his time as a young student and the wonderful days he spent in San Marino. At that moment, Tacchi did everything possible to persuade Lieutenant Colonel Christiani to abandon the operation. They informed Christiani about the anti-British sentiment among the people of San Marino and noted that the British had just bombed them. Furthermore, they pointed out that over 70,000 refugees were present in San Marino at that time. They added that the propaganda would negatively impact Germany if they violated the neutrality of the small Republic. At that point, Christiani called one of his superiors. He might have spoken to Kesselring himself; then he hung up and said, "*All postponed.*"[160]

But on August 28th, the anti-Fascists killed a Turkmen soldier near the border of Cerbaiola and soon after took refuge within the territory of San Marino. The Germans dispatched some soldiers to the area of Fiorentino, where they took 10 hostages, 8 of whom were San Marino citizens. They were all taken to the town hall in Montegrimano, where they would be shot, according to German orders stating that German soldiers had to be avenged at a 10 to 1 ratio.

---

160. From the interview with Amedeo Montemaggi, Rimini.

The Government of San Marino, represented by Federico Bigi, strongly complained to the German command. As a result, the Germans proposed a so-called "barter", meaning they intended to exchange the 10 prisoners in Montegrimano for 10 "unwelcome" Italian citizens who had sought refuge in San Marino. Bigi continued his mediation, and the prisoners were released three days later under the guarantee that no anti-Fascist action would start from San Marino.[161]

On August 25, 1944, Winston Churchill gave the order to begin the final assault on the Gothic Line. General Alexander launched an unprecedented attack from the banks of the Metauro River.

On August 30, a pincer movement closed in on the German defenses, and 1,200,000 soldiers fought a relentless battle on the field during the 21 days that followed.

The last inhabitants of the towns located in the vicinity of the Line were ordered to abandon their homes within two hours. At that point, the Germans directed everyone towards San Marino, and suddenly, the number of displaced people increased to 100,000.[162]

Rimini, already battered by almost a year of aerial bombings, was hit by 1,470,000 cannon shots, 11,510 air missions, and an unspecified number of long-range projectiles fired from the warships anchored offshore. Some of these even reached Borgo Maggiore. The fields at the foot of Mount Titano were filled with cattle placed there by displaced farmers: it was a safe place, or so they thought.[163] The cows were all killed. But it was not only the animals that died. There were also 201 civilian victims, 86 of whom were from San Marino. In Montegiardino, a cannon shot grazed the Captain Regent, Sanzio Valentini, who was wounded, while the two young soldiers escorting him, along with a civilian who just happened to be passing by, were

---

161. From the newspaper *Il Resto del Carlino,* August 18, 1956 "Il Baratto," interview with Francesco Balsimelli.

162. Amedeo Montemaggi – Itinerari della Linea Gotica 1944. Guida storico iconografica ai campi di battaglia (Itineraries of the Gothic Line 1944. Historical-Iconographic guide of the battle fields) – 2010 ed. Museo dell'Aviazione – Rimini.

163. From the interview with Bruno Ghigi, Rimini.

The Highlanders' parade.
— Photo by MW, Republic of San Marino. —

killed. The streets were invaded by retreating German tanks, which scattered a myriad of mines behind them. At the end of the battle, 80,000 civilian and military victims were counted along what had been the Gothic Line.

On September 23, there was a large parade of Scottish Highlanders on Liberty Square. Harold MacMillan, the Minister Resident for Great Britain in the Mediterranean, and General Sir Oliver Leese, Commander of the Eighth British Army, arrived at the Public Palace for the liberation ceremony. The people of San Marino did not appreciate it much, as they had never truly been occupied. While the bagpipes were marching by, someone claimed to have heard Captain Regent Francesco Balsimelli exclaim, *"in slà fnesc piò sa sta piva?"*[164] (when will they stop making all that noise with those pipes?), while artillery shots could still be heard coming from the north. Three days later, the ceremony was repeated, and this time General Harold Alexander arrived.

The Highlanders' parade.
— Photo by MW, Republic of San Marino. —

164. From the interview with Giuseppina Tamagnini, RSM.

The Highlanders' parade.
– Photo by MW, Republic of San Marino. –

Another moment of the great parade: in the middle is Captain Regent Francesco Balsimelli turning his back to the military authorities.
– Photo by MW, Republic of San Marino. –

Balsimelli, who was offended that Alexander expected to meet some sort of "Mayor," made him wait for two hours. He then asked the Master of Ceremonies to inform the General that "he was now ready to meet him"[165] and to explain to him that a "Captain Regent is a President."

On that day, two interesting things occurred that are relevant to this story. According to some friends of his, Federico Bigi took Alexander on a tour of the old town center following the ceremony. The last point of interest he wished to show Alexander was the Convent of Saint Francis, not for its significance as a historical work of art, but because of the Jews sheltered by Father Cesari. It is said that the General was astonished when he saw all those people. The second fact was recounted by Celio Gozi in his memoir: *"A commission of Jews led by Otto Ruhl immediately approached the Anglo-American Command to seek respect and salvation for the former Fascist rulers of San Marino, recognizing their generous and humane gestures towards them."*[166]

There is no trace of this meeting in any documents, apart from Giuliano Gozi's personal diary, as quoted by his brother but not proven. However, it can be assumed that it really did occur. On November 3, 1944, Major Zervudachi, the Political Liaison Officer of the Allied Army, wrote a letter to the Secretaries of State to distance himself from the arrest of seven Fascists from San Marino, among whom were Giuliano and Manlio Gozi. He explained that it had been "an internal measure which did not involve the Allied Command."

---

165. Registry Office of the Republic of San Marino.

166. Celio Gozi, *Memoria sugli Ebrei a San Marino durante l'ultimo conflitto* (Memorial about the Jews in San Marino during the recent conflict) – Gozi's Collection, RSM.

Ufficiale Politico di Collegamento
San Marino

3 Novembre 1944.

Alla Segreteria di Stato
San Marino

OGGETTO: Arresti in casa.

Io desidero che sia chiaro, in seguito alla nostra conversazione di stamattina, che il Comando Alleato, rappresentato qui da me stesso, non ha nessun motivo valido di sicurezza per raccomandare la continuazione dell'arresto in casa delle seguenti persone:

GOZI GIULIANO
GOZI MANLIO
FOSCHI SALVATORE
ROSSI GIUSEPPE
BRASCHI ANTONIO
BRASCHI ARRIGO
BALSIMELLI ARTURO

Desidero che sia inteso, perciò, che se il provvedimento contro queste persone sarà continuato esso rappresenterà intieramente una misura interna che non coinvolge il Comando Alleato.

(F°) L.E.Zervudachi
Major.

Letter by Major Zervudachi
— Courtesy of the State Archives of the Republic of San Marino; Ezio Balducci Archive. —

Political Liaison Officer
with
San Marino

November 3, 1944

To the Secretariat of State
of San Marino

Subject: House arrests

I want to make it clear that, following our conversation this morning, the Allied Command, represented by me here, has no valid security reason to recommend the house arrest of the following people:

GOZI, GIULIANO
GOZI, MANLIO
FOSCHI, SALVATORE
ROSSI, GIUSEPPE
BRASCHI, ANTONIO
BRASCHI, ARRIGO
BALSIMELLI, ARTURO

Therefore, I also want to point out that if the provisions against the individuals mentioned above continue, they will be considered an internal measure that does not involve the Allied Command.

L.E. Zeravudachi
Major

THE LAST ACT

The day of reckoning came immediately. The peace pact that had saved the Republic was soon forgotten. On September 23, in his speech to the Great and General Council, Balsimelli stated: *"It may be that our political conduct, often made up of prudence and foresight... has not fully been to everyone's satisfaction, but to the skeptics of every kind, to the critics in bad faith, to the opponents taking a stand on principle, to the intransigent to the bitter end, to the spreaders of rumors, to the draft dodgers, to the heroes of the last minute, to the enthusiasts of the past, and to the future deluded we say with certainty that we have acted in the best interest of the nation."*[167]

When the Gozis were arrested, Balducci's last mission had been completed. Giuliano Gozi, with whom he had worked side by side for a year without ever looking into his eyes, the man who had forced him into exile, was now in prison. The war was over, and the country was safe. On November 1, 1944, Balducci handed in his letter of resignation to the Captains Regent: "My duties have ceased with the onset of war events and my conscience and sensitivity require me today to return my mandate to Their Excellencies and to the Council whom I would like to thank for the trust given to me during this year's hard-fought battle for the freedom of our homeland."[168]

---

167. From the speech given by Captain Regent Francesco Balsimelli to the Great and General Council on 09-23-1944.

168. Ezio Balducci Archive; letter to the Captains Regent dated November 1, 1944 (State Archives, RSM).

San Marino 28 Sett. 944 - 1643 d.F.R.
Ill.mo Sig. Maggiore
La Signora Regina Grimpert-Brambilla, di nazionalità Polacca, di razza ebraica, rifugiata a San Marino e protetta nonostante tutto per il principio sacrosanto del diritto d'asilo a tutti i perseguitati, desidera da lei alcune informazioni; se mi compiacerà intenderò questo come un atto di gentilezza fatto a me.
Con più distinti ossequi
Francesco Balsimelli
Al Maggiore Zervudaki - Ufficiale di Collegamento
Palazzo

Dott. Prof. Francesco Balsimelli

Note by Captain Regent Francesco Balsimelli to Major Zervudachi from September 28, 1944 written on Balsimelli's letter-headed paper.

San Marino, September 28, 1944-1643 D.F.R.[169]

Dear Major,

Mrs. Regina Grymberg Brambilla, a Polish national of Jewish descent, who has taken refuge in San Marino and has been protected in accordance with the most sacred right of asylum extended to all victims of persecution, would like to request some information from you. Should you kindly fulfill this request, I will regard it as a favor done to me.

Yours sincerely,

Francesco Balsimelli

To Major Zervudachi, Liaison Officer

Palace

169. This acronym means "Since the foundation of the Republic," and it is still used today to date official documents [translator's note].

The time when "he navigated between Scylla and Charybdis," as Balsimelli said, was behind him. Daily life in San Marino went on as usual. The advance of the Allies slowed down in the vicinity of Cesena, but it resumed to the north soon after. The Border Militia was dissolved, and Giorgio Zani and Maria José Mandelli went back to their bantering and playing dirty tricks on each other: "I remember one day he tied me to the window, "she said, "people passed by and laughed...I was wearing some underwear...yes, my grandmother's long underwear."[170] In those years, he had bred a cow and was very proud of it. The Zani family had a house in the countryside, and Zani would occasionally take his friends to see his "cow Paolina." One day, Maria José, with the complicity of Giorgio's father, pulled a beautiful white raincoat from his closet and embroidered a large inscription on the back: "Long live cow Paolina." She placed the article of clothing back into the closet and waited.

Giorgio Zani happened to wear his "embroidered" coat at a ceremony marking the return of electric power. Also, thanks to his involvement, the power stations destroyed by the Germans had been restored. He arrived in Liberty Square, proud and satisfied, but something was wrong: the people around him could hardly hold back their laughter, which erupted shortly after. When he discovered why they were laughing, he looked around for the culprit. "*He knew immediately that it was my doing,*" she said, "*I was on the other side of the square when he began to run towards me. He chased me all the way home, where I locked myself in. I remember that I didn't go out for a month. Then, tons of letters began to arrive: they were all marriage proposals. That nasty guy had placed an ad in a newspaper in Rome... girl from a good family... with a slight physical defect... is searching for her soul mate. Even my father got angry that time.*"[171] Zani pointed out: "*I didn't place any ad. My friends at the military school in Rome helped me out.*"[172] She continued: "*And think that my father would have approved of a marriage between me and Giorgio. We were so*

170. From the interview with Maria José Mandelli, Reggio Calabria.

171. Ibid.

172. From the interview with Attorney Giorgio Zani, RSM.

crazy instead... He chased after me from the square up to my house. If he had gotten hold of me, he would have beaten the living daylights out of me... I ran all the way down the street in record time... but do you know which street I'm talking about?" "Yes, Viale Antonio Onofri!" *"No, we used to call it Rose Avenue... because it was always full of roses."*

Here follows a short story, which Francesco Balsimelli wrote and printed on his own, dedicated to little Edoardo Brambilla.

At the top, there is a dedication written by Balsimelli in Polish, another language he studied. I was told by a native speaker that there are some errors in the dedication, but the meaning was supposed to be the following:

"To the little ugly man from his first teacher, in the hope that he will never forget him; signed, the big ugly man."

San Marino, August 1946

HI THERE!

He looked like a yapping puppy, and every time he saw soldiers climbing the steep slope leading to the Fortress, he would run toward them from the terrace, screaming, "Hi there!" Edzio was not yet five years old: a cross between Latin and Slavic blood, a mixture of Jewish and Aryan races, a prodigy of intelligence.

He spoke Polish, his mother's language, and Italian, contaminated by a few sentences in dialect learned from the other children around him.

He had learned to bid his farewells in English, which earned him some chocolate bars or chewing gum: "Hi there!"

One day, four officers and a sergeant passed by. They wore a badge of the orzel (eagle) on their caps; on their left sleeve, they had a white and red shield featuring a pine tree:

it was the symbol of the divizia karpacka. They also had a red semicircle on their epaulettes with a word written in white letters: Poland.

Until then, only Brits, New Zealanders, Canadians, South Africans, and Indians had passed through there. Edzio, who did not know how to read, made no distinction between them; to him, they were all English, so he repeated the usual refrain: "Hi there!".

Among the four soldiers stood the captain, who stopped short, struck by that blue-eyed little boy with flowing golden curls. He smiled and pulled a packet of biscuits from his pocket. He spoke without the slightest hope of being understood: "Nie: By By, dziecko; dzien dobry, rozumiesz?".

Edzio fell from the clouds, but the Carpathian Division officer was even more shocked when he heard the boy respondinging with an excited voice: *"Rozumien, rozumien, panie; bardzo dzienkuje!"*. Then he jumped down the steep steps screaming in a voice as high as a piccolo: *"Mamo, kodz; Polacy! Polacy!"*

The captain called the others over, and everyone, amazed and curious, followed the boy who had climbed the stairway of his house. He beat on the door with his fists and kicked it at the same time while shouting as loud as he could: "Otworz, mamo, Predko, Polacy!".

Before his mother opened the door, the four officers were on the landing. She did not understand what was going on, and exasperated by her son's insistence, who was drumming on the door, she moved to open it, shouting in a threatening tone: "Cicho badz!" — When...

The scene was extremely touching.

It was the first time Polish soldiers had arrived in this country, which had been freed just a couple of weeks earlier. The woman was shocked, but even more surprised were the officers who had heard words in their language first coming from the child's mouth and now from his mother's, who was flushed with joy and excitement.

Her compatriots introduced themselves, and each one kissed her hand.

"Prosze, Panowie, prosze" — she said enthusiastically, inviting them in.

The modest yet pretty house had a narrow entranceway that served as a small sitting room on certain occasions. There was a wicker table with four chairs of the same material, and lying on the floor was a carpet made from the skin of a magnificent tiger. The room was small, and there were very few chairs. The dining room was cluttered with trunks and was not accessible. She led her unexpected guests to a larger, more charming, and intimate room.

The captain was the first to walk in, and when their hostess apologized for the room, he replied gallantly that there could be no more inviting place than a beautiful woman's bedroom. She sat limply on the edge of the low-rise twentieth-century double bed placed in the middle of the room. Next to that piece of furniture were Edzio's bed, a dresser, a vanity, and a closet. There was still enough space for the chairs on which the officers and the sergeant, who came a little later, sat. Plenty of light and air flowed into the two windows, while the curtains billowed like sails in the afternoon breeze of the first few days of October.

Edzio was really excited. He moved from the captain's lap to the sergeant's and drowned out everybody's voices with his screams. He was amazed that these tall men did not speak or understand po wlosku, while he could speak Italian and Polish even though he was just a child.

They had been in Italy for a few months. They had followed the Allied army to Africa and fought in Marmarica, Cyrenaica, and Tripolitania. They told them about the hasty retreat of the Wehrmacht, which had used all the vehicles available, leaving the Italian troops without any means of transport. They had landed in Sicily, moved on to Taranto, and then marched up the peninsula, sowing death on the route. They had finally occupied Cassino, hunting out the last German resistance with their bayonets and grenades among the ruins left by the RAF. Then continued north, up to the Gothic Line, to the Foglia, Conca and Marano rivers, three waterways that had made a name for themselves thanks to the German resistance and the Allies' caution. Forget about learning Italian...

The cannons were now thundering beyond the Marecchia and Senio rivers, and the battle to conquer Bologna was raging.

Leese and Alexander had passed through; rattling along the slopes of Mount Titano were endless rows of tanks and roaring columns of motor vehicles, motorized trailers, and the vast array of resources that the Allies were utilizing to wear down the tenacious resistance of the enemy.

Soldiers of every race and color now flocked there like tourists. They rested after so much hard work and before the next battle. Each had sacks and backpacks full of cigarettes, soap, and canned food, which they traded or exchanged for wine and spirits.

The captain nodded to the sergeant, who went to retrieve the knapsack he had left in the entranceway. He opened it and began to take out all sorts of good things.

Edzio opened his eyes wide with curiosity and satisfaction. "Dla mnie?" – he cried every time the sergeant, like a magician, pulled out a can of beef, fish, milk, coffee, tea, sugarloaf, and chocolate. "Drziekuie." Then, turning to his mother, he said, "Pan bardzo dobry jest!" For him, they were not officers; they were friends. He spoke to them informally and called them by their first names: Josio, Domeiko, Mietek, Piotre.

The woman thanked them with emotion and insisted on offering them a cup of the tea they had given her: *"Filizanke Herbaty"* — and she went into the kitchen.

"Kto to jest?" the captain asked the boy.

His eyes were fixed on a large photograph on the vanity table. The picture depicted a young man in a colonial-style outfit, consisting of a bush jacket and shorts; his gaze was directed towards a distant country where he had left his heart.

The soldier spelled out and articulated the syllables of the dedication written in a corner, but he did so without understanding its meaning: "To... my... "

"To jest moj dad," replied the boy.

"Gdzie znajduje sie?"

Edzio traced a sign with his hand and, sighing deeply, said, "Daleko, daleko!"

Captain Domeiko placed the little blonde boy on his lap and, holding onto his head, stared at him emotionally.

"Dziecko but niebieskie oczy tak jak moj wladzio," he said to his colleagues. He, too, had a child of that age, with the same big blue eyes. He had left him with his mother in Palestine. He was just a baby the last time he saw him. He pulled a recent photograph out of his wallet. It showed a small child laughing while standing up and waving his hand, as if to greet his father, who was far away.

"Ladny the madry tak jak ty." He is as cute and smart as you are, said the soldier, showing the picture to Edzio. His voice had become shaky. He covered his face with his hands. Edzio wanted to uncover those wet eyes, and tried in vain to separate the captain's hands: *"Dla czego placzesz?"* Why are you crying?

The others were silent, and so was the mother, who had come in with a tray and a steaming teapot without saying a word. She opened her mouth just to say, "Oto, here you are."

In that brief moment of silence, they heard confused voices outside, followed by the noisy and heavy sound of marching boots walking up the steep stairway leading to the Fortress.

Edzio quickly slipped off the captain's lap, climbed onto a chair to reach the windowsill, and, making a megaphone with his hands, shouted "Hi there!"

Edoardo Brambilla Grymberg and one of the Polish soldiers he met again a few years later in Milan.
— Courtesy of Edoardo Brambilla Grymberg. —

RETURN

Otto Ruhl and his wife Rosa were among the first to leave San Marino, but they did not return to Milan immediately; the situation there was still too sticky.

Celio Gozi and his son Guidubaldo met up with them in Pesaro. They were seated at a table in a café on Via Rossini: "As soon as they saw us, they quickly got up and joyfully came up and embraced us affectionately."[173]

Mr. and Mrs. Ruhl sent a letter with their best wishes to San Marino during the Christmas holidays of 1946. By that time, they had moved to Milan. Coincidentally, Manlio Gozi, the former secretary of the San Marino Fascist Party, and his family had also relocated to Milan. Gozi had spent a year in prison before being exiled, and his apartment had been given to Professor Emiliani by the government authorities. "My father went to visit the professor," said Gian Piero Gozi, "and told him he was there to get the furniture; it was very valuable, and he did not want him to take it away. My father insisted, telling him that the furniture belonged to him. He managed to get 30,000 liras for it. It was everything we had, and with that money, we moved to Milan. In the early days, we lived in a basement.[174] Then, Ruhl's letter changed their lives. Gozi found a job thanks to him, once they got back into touch with each other. During his career, he had

173. Celio Gozi, *Memoria sugli Ebrei a San Marino durante l'ultimo conflitto* (Memorial about the Jews in San Marino during the recent conflict) – Gozi's Collection, RSM.

174. From the interview with Gian Piero Gozi, RSM.

RUHL,
presso KARTRO S.A.I.
Via Andrea Doria 7
MILANO.

Milano 20 dicembre 1946.

Gentile Signora Clizia,

per darVi occasione di ricordarci, ci permettiamo inviarVi l'acclusa piccola fotografia veramente ben riuscita.

Noi speriamo che, tanto Voi quanto il Vostro preg. cognato Conte Gozzi, stiate bene.

In occasione delle prossome Feste di Natale e Capodanno, Vi preghiamo gradire i nostri più cordiali auguri ed il voto che l'anno 1947 abbia ad apportarVi salute, gioia e successo.

Dato che per il momento non è possibile fare nulla per il nostro viaggio in Brasile, seguiteremo a stare a Milano.

Abbiamo saputo che il Signor Manlio si troverebbe a Milano con la sua famiglia e gradiremmo avere il suo indirizzo per poter fargli una visita, sempre però beninteso che questo non gli rechi disturbo.

Con i nostri piu cordiali saluti ed il più riconoscente ricordo, sempre

Vostri
Rosa e Otto Ruhl

The letter written by the Ruhls to Clizia Gozi during Christmas holidays in 1946.
— Courtesy of the State Archives of the Republic of San Marino; Gozi's Collection. —

RUHL
At KARTRO S.A.I. Milan, December 20, 1946
Via Andrea Doria 7
MILAN

Dear Clizia,

Please find herewith attached a particularly well-taken picture to remind you of us.

We hope that you and your dear brother-in-law, Count Gozi, are well.

We wish you a Merry Christmas and a Happy New Year. We hope 1947 will bring health, joy and success to you.

As at present we cannot carry on with the plans for our trip to Brazil, we will continue to stay in Milan.

We have learnt that Manlio is also here in Milan with his family. We would like to have his address in order to pay him a visit, unless it is a bother for him, of course.

With our fondest greetings and grateful memory.

Yours sincerely,
Rosa and Otto Ruhl

been the "Secretary of the Fascist Party," but at that time, the word "Fascist" was not a good omen, especially in the city where his Italian counterpart had been hanged upside down. Manlio Gozi began working as a salesman for the company Kartro. He only stayed there for six months selling sheets of carbon paper with Ruhl, but he learned the job, which he continued doing for other prestigious companies.

CAMILLO CASTIGLIONI

Roma, 1° ottobre 1957

Carissimo Alvaro,

non ho potuto rispondere prima alla tua del 25 u. s. perchè ho avuto durante tutta la settimana un attacco fortissimo che ha stremato le mie forze, ma ho potuto telefonare con due Ministeri, specialmente con quello degli Esteri, dove ho degli amici fidatissimi e mi hanno assicurato di aver richiamato il Console Generale a Roma proprio per mettere le cose in ordine e che l'Italia non si lascierà turlupinare proprio all'interno del suo Paese.
Questo corrisponde a quanto ti avevo consigliato e cioè di venire subito a Roma, assicurandoti che in questo caso tutto verrebbe messo a posto. Questa notte ho inteso le prime notizie secondo le quali tu eri stato messo a capo della Milizia e sono sicuro che tu ora saprai battere i pugni sul tavolo e mostrare a questa gente chi sei. Io che ti ho visto fresco e tranquillo con una palla al cuore, non dubito un momento che adesso mostrerai i denti a questa gente, che ha avuto il coraggio di gridarti: fascista. Ma guarda che devi tener duro e non devi chiudere nemmeno un occhio, perchè sono certissimo che proveranno ancora ogni sorta di trucchi per imbrogliarvi o per mettervi dalla parte del torto.
Sarebbe ridicolo che in questo momento, nel quale non saprai dove dar la testa, io ti domandi di scrivermi, cercherò di telefonarti e spero di riuscire.
Ringraziate Iddio che tutto per il momento sembra andar bene e non mollate, per carità, NON MOLLATE!
In questo momento tu sai che sono uno dei pochissimi che sente con te, profondamente con te, colla mente e col cuore.
Dì alla tua famiglia che mi felicito con loro ed anzitutto col mio carissimo Libero. Ti abbraccio.

C. C.

Dott. Alvaro Casali
San Marino

Camillo Castiglioni's last letter to Alvaro Casali. The "Rovereta events" had already occurred.
— Courtesy of Aroldo Casali – Republic of San Marino. —

After finally abandoning his Franciscan habit, a symbol of absolute poverty, Camillo Castiglioni returned to wearing his pure cashmere outfits. In winter 1945, he asked Alvaro Casali to drive him to Rome. He still had a beautiful villa in the elegant Parioli[175] district, but he did not stay there very long. He spent long periods at the Hotel Regina in Viareggio, gazing at the sea and blue sky.

Businesses and big speculations were merely a memory of the past, or nearly so. Under strong pressure, he brokered a joint venture worth a billion dollars between the American Rothschild and Tito's Yugoslavia. He then wrote countless letters to his friend Casali, consistently offering him ample political advice for the welfare of the small Republic of San Marino. He returned to Mount Titano several times, trying to convince Rockefeller to accompany him as well. However, the local politicians of that period did not encourage such a visit, fearing that a man of his status could buy the whole country. Castiglioni's relationship with the Italian politicians during the riots in 1957, when the left-wing government was overthrown in San Marino, is clearly documented in his letters. He subsequently intervened with his English friends to assist San Marino in obtaining indemnity for the damages caused by the bombing on June 26, 1944. Indeed, Britain did send a total of £70,000 in 1960, but in the form of a "contribution" and not "compensation." However, Camillo Castiglioni never saw that day. He died in Rome on December 18, 1957, without ever revealing where he had sought refuge during the crucial stages of the Second World War.

This (image on pg. 174) is the last letter written by Camillo Castiglioni to Alvaro Casali before his death. Castiglioni tells him that he does not feel well at all and feels very weak, yet he is extremely worried about the news he has received from San Marino, where the political disorders known as the "Rovereta events" are taking place.

In the central part of the letter, Castiglioni writes about the days he spent in San Marino:

---

175. From the interview with Aroldo Casali, RSM.

"I saw you grow up with a bullet lodged right near your heart."

He is referring to the attempt on Alvaro Casali's life on February 6, 1944, thus confirming his presence in San Marino at that time.

As soon as the war ended, Salvatore Donati, together with his uncle Angelo, returned to San Marino while Salvatore's wife and children remained in Switzerland until they finished their studies.[176]

Salvatore may have wanted to see what had happened after his departure, and he was probably curious to know if it had been worth all the risks he took during that adventurous journey to find refuge there. His company in Modena had been completely destroyed by the bombings, so he collaborated with two men in his business, one from Rimini and the other from San Marino, to establish a tannery in Acquaviva on November 16, 1945. Its name was "Società Anonima Conceria e Calzaturificio Sammarinese' (San Marino Tannery and Shoe Factory Corporation).[177]

At the beginning, it functioned very well, but on January 22, 1951, Salvatore Donati died at the age of 49. The other two partners lacked Donati's knowledge and ability, and after a few years, the company went bankrupt.

During the same trip at the end of 1945, Angelo Donati was honored with the title of "Knight of St. Agatha" and appointed "Charge d'Affaires in Paris for the Republic of San Marino." In 1953, he became "Minister Plenipotentiary." In that same year, Donati played a key role alongside Pope John XXIII, his friend since the days when Angelo Roncalli served as Apostolic Nuncio to Paris, in the resolution of the famous "Affair Finaly."[178] In that case, two Jewish orphans were saved by some Catholic sisters. At the end of the war, they did not want to return the children to their aunts and uncles because they had been baptized in the meantime.

---

176. CDEC – Milan, "Personal Vicissitude" section, letter written by Amedeo Donati.

177. Celio Gozi, *Memoria sugli Ebrei a San Marino durante l'ultimo conflitto* (Memorial about the Jews in San Marino during the recent conflict) – Gozi's Collection, RSM.

178. Paolo Veneziano, quoted work.

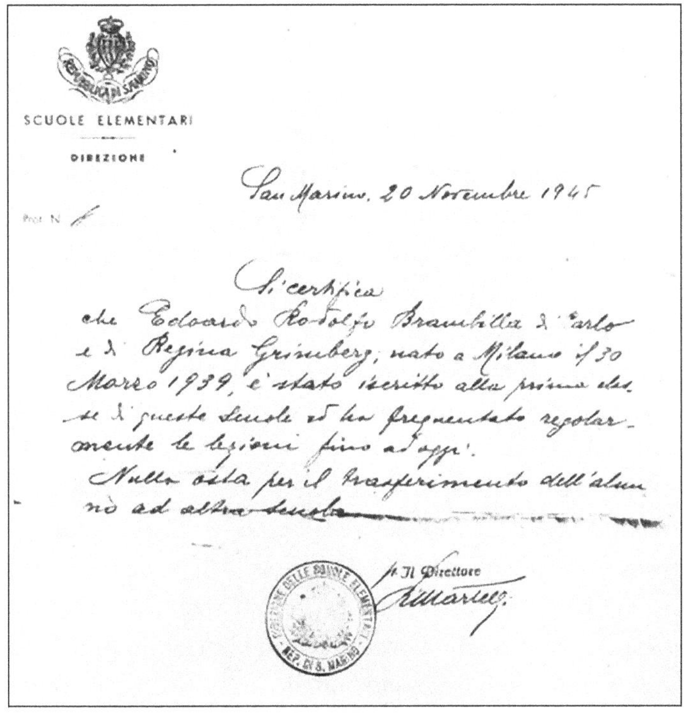

SCUOLE ELEMENTARI

DIREZIONE

Prot. N. 6

San Marino, 20 Novembre 1945

Si certifica
che Edoardo Rodolfo Brambilla di Carlo
e di Regina Grimberg, nato a Milano il 30
Marzo 1939, è stato iscritto alla prima clas-
se di queste scuole ed ha frequentato regolar-
mente le lezioni fino ad oggi.
Nulla osta per il trasferimento dell'alun-
no ad altra scuola

DIREZIONE DELLE SCUOLE ELEMENTARI REP. DI S. MARINO

p. Il Direttore
Martelli

Edoardo Brambilla's school certificate on letter-headed paper of the Administration Office of the Elementary School of San Marino.
– Courtesy of Edoardo Brambilla Grymberg. –

San Marino November 20, 1945

It is hereby certified that Edoardo Rodolfo Brambilla, son of Carlo Brambilla and Regina Grymberg, born in Milan on March 30, 1939, is enrolled in first grade at this school and has regularly attended lessons up to today.

There is no impediment to the transfer of the pupil to another school.

Seal of the Administration Office of
the Elementary School of San Marino
Martelli, Principal

Angelo Donati died in 1960 at the age of 76. On January 26, 2004, the Gold Medal for Civil Merit was awarded in his memory.

Many people gathered to greet Regina Grymberg on the day of her departure. A man from Milan came to pick her up; some believed he was her husband. In reality, he was just a neighbor who came to lend a hand. He introduced himself to Raffaele Amati, the owner of the apartment where the family had lived throughout their stay in San Marino. Grymberg's friend was quite concerned, as he thought he would have to pay for the woman's rent and did not have much money on him. Amati told him not to worry because he did not owe him anything. Some say that Francesco Balsimelli settled the amount due for Regina Grymberg's rent.

When they arrived in Milan, they found a strange sign on the door of their house at Via Cesare Mangili, 2. The local authorities had given that building to some homeless people, believing that the family who had lived there was all dead. Three years after the end of the war, Carlo Brambilla was finally able to embrace his reunited family. Edoardo had his hair cut and did not want to eat tripe again. Among the dearest memories he has jealously guarded since then is the original text of the last speech given by Francesco Balsimelli to the Great and General Council as Captain Regent on September 23, 1944.

Giancarlo Bonfiglioli announced to his friends that he would return home. Giuseppe Mandelli asked his daughter, Maria José, to go to the Convent and bring him something to eat during the trip. She prepared a couple of lunch bags and, as requested by her father, took them to their friend. Surprised by such kindness, he asked the girl if he could accompany her back home. That walk, which lasted only a few minutes, seemed like a simple, polite gesture, but Bonfiglioli viewed it as a promise of engagement. However, Maria José did not see it the same way. "I met Giancarlo after some time on the streets of Bologna. He insulted me because I did not get in touch with him at all after that walk. He was really rude!"[179]

179. From the interview with Maria José Mandelli, Reggio Calabria.

Armando Russi left as well, but not to go to his native Ancona. According to Celio Gozi, he went to live in Turin, where he married a Roman Catholic elementary school teacher, with whom he had a daughter. Then nothing more was heard about either him or his father's cousins, Emilia and Elisa Rossi.[180]

Erma Hendl did not return to Merano with her elderly mother, Malvina Kohn. Instead, they went to live in Bologna, on via Faustino Malaguti at number 11. Nothing more was known about the two women until 1981. In fact, on September 29 of that year, Erma died. Following her will, the Golfieri Funeral Home in Bologna took her remains to the cemetery of Montalbo, in San Marino, where she was buried next to her husband, Franco Lo Monaco.[181]

The woman named Carlotta never had either a last name or a precise origin in San Marino. She was and would always be "the German lady." Today, many believe that she was a Jew, but there is no evidence confirming this, partly because no one remembers her last name. What is certain is that the woman was nasty and really gutsy, but even so, all the young men wanted her as their mother-in-law. In fact, it seems that someone went to put some flowers on her grave in the small cemetery of Campo Tures, a few kilometers from the Austrian border.[182]

The entire country had fallen in love with her daughter, Edith, whose angelic face and long blond hair were often worn either loose or tied up in a long braid. Yet, in the end, she broke everybody's heart by leaving San Marino with an Australian soldier!

"There was no way my father would leave San Marino," said Maria José Mandelli, but my mother won the war between husband

---

180. Celio Gozi, *Memoria sugli Ebrei a San Marino durante l'ultimo conflitto* (Memorial about the Jews in San Marino during the recent conflict) – Gozi's Collection, RSM.

181. Registry Office of the Republic of San Marino.

182. After the first edition of this book, Davide Bagnaresi from the University of Bologna has found the name of the two women: Charlotte Neuendorf, born in Berlin, and her daughter Edith Reuter, Conference "San Marino terra di giusti" (San Marino, land of the righteous), January 27, 2013, Fondazione Valori Tattili – Asset Banca, RSM.

The sign that Regina Grymberg found on the door of her house in Milan.
— Courtesy of Edoardo Brambilla Grymberg. —

and wife: Edith Grünfeld wanted her children to go back to school in Bologna. Moreover, Giuseppe Mandelli had inherited a beautiful house on Via Farini from his mother, where they went to live together with the old Grünfelds. Bettina died on November 6, 1952, and Leopold followed her footsteps two months later, on January 18, 1953. They were both buried in the Certosa Cemetery in Bologna. Maria José married a young man from Sicily when she was 24. He had studied chemistry at the University of Bologna, and by sheer coincidence, he took her to live in Reggio Calabria, the city where both Giorgio Zani and Attilio Balsimelli, the man who kept the children hidden in the cellar during the fall of 1943, were born. Maria José still lives there and is a supporter of her young granddaughter, a future Italian star on the tennis courts.

The youngest daughter of the Mandelli family, Patrizia Marina, returned to San Marino many times. She went to visit her nanny, the one who had let go of the stroller during the bombings on June 26, 1944. Her name was Elena, and she was from Chiesanuova.

Her aunt Zita also returned to Bologna. She and her husband, Mario Guizzardi, gave their house in San Marino to a young chemist named Attilio Caramaschi, an employee of the Colorificio Sammarinese, who would soon become the company manager. Mario Guizzardi died in October 1980 in a tragic car accident during one of his many trips between the Colorificio and Bologna. Today, the company he founded is among the most important in San Marino.

The descendants of Simone Michelotti still manage "La Serenissima," the San Marino cake factory. They are preparing to celebrate the seventieth anniversary of the business and proudly continue to use the same original wafer griddles, which have been duly restored. Surely now, after so long, we can say without a shadow of a doubt that the wafer is a typical product of San Marino, although it is now produced almost everywhere.

After the war, Giuseppe Nicolini kept the promise he made to Giuliano Gozi. One day, he took the train to Venice with a suitcase full of gold ingots to return them to their rightful owner: "My father was very disappointed," said Carla Nicolini, "Marco Ara neither thanked him nor bothered to offer to pay for his train ticket."[183]

From the left: Edoardo, Carlo Brambilla, and his wife Regina Grymberg.
— Courtesy of Edoardo Brambilla Grymberg. —

183. From the interview with Carla Nicolini, RSM.

Gerard Richard Gumpert was captured by the Allied troops and held as a witness at the Nuremberg trial. He remained in a building within the American camp in Ludwigsburg until the end of 1947; then, he was transferred to one in Stuttgart. It is said that he knew all the secrets about the surrender negotiations between the Germans and the Allies. He maintained his correspondence with Balducci from prison.[184]

When he was released in January 1949, Gumpert wanted to return to Italy, but he still could not obtain a visa because he was a German citizen. Therefore, Balducci secured a residence permit for him in San Marino, where he lived and where his two children were born. For his first job, he began exporting Lambretta motorbikes to Germany, and then he decided to import Volkswagen Beetle cars into Italy. He founded a company in Verona named Autogerma, which was the exclusive importer of Volkswagen cars in Italy. In 1963, the German playwright Rolf Ochhuth wrote the play "The Vicar," inspired by the letter sent by the fake Pope written by Gumpert. The performance of this play was banned in Italy because it did not comply with the Concordat provisions. The same work was used as a pretext by the Jewish community to halt the process of beatification of Pius XII.

The former Fascist leader Giuliano Gozi went to Rome after being exiled from San Marino. He was employed in the Vatican as a clerk, thanks to Father Alfredo Caesari's acquaintances. He worked on organizing the 1950 Holy Year but did not stay long in Rome due to his poor health. A few years later, he received permission to return to San Marino, but he was prohibited from working there as a lawyer. He did so anyway, using the name and seal of Guidubaldo Gozi, his favorite nephew, who had graduated in law. Giuliano Gozi died in 1965.

After the war, Ezio Balducci wanted to give up his political commitment and work as a full-time doctor. However, he was

184. Ezio Balducci Archive. Gumpert's letters to Balducci dated March 24, 1947; November 16, 1947; December 17, 1947; December 20, 1947; December 22, 1947; December 31, 1948, State Archives, RSM.

strongly urged from different fronts to remain in politics, so he accepted and became an "independent" candidate on the lists of the San Marino Christian Democratic Party. He was elected for two consecutive legislatures. He died prematurely in Rome on January 30, 1957, at the age of 53. Among the hundreds of memories and stories that one may hear or read about Balducci, there is one that reveals his true personality. The story comes from Dr. Ferruccio Piva and refers to the years after the war: "*I remember one night there was a party in Serravalle. It was a private event with several high-ranking people, like today's VIPs, so the young people, including us, had been excluded from the list of invitations. We decided to barricade the way out of the house with stones, iron bars and wooden poles. While we got down to work on it, suddenly Ezio Balducci came along. He had been invited to the party and when he saw us, he asked what we were doing and why. After being told, he turned right around and exclaimed: "If that's the case, then carry on with it!"*"

On March 25, 1960, the main street in the town of Serravalle was dedicated to Ezio Balducci. Even today, you can hear about a couple of silver candelabra, located in an unspecified home, that were given to Balducci by a Jew who had sought refuge in San Marino.

Paolo Tacchi, the Fascist Federal of Rimini, at times a friend and at times a terror of San Marino, escaped from Rimini on August 30, 1944. He was captured in Como in the spring of 1945 and imprisoned in Procida (Naples). He underwent a trial in Forlì, where he was accused of the murder of the three Martyrs of Rimini. He was sentenced to death in 1946 but acquitted on appeal in 1949 for not having committed the crime. Tacchi himself, in fact, did not hang the three young anti-Fascists; the German soldiers did. He underwent six more trials for minor offenses, but he was never imprisoned again. In 1964, he returned to San Marino to ask the government for official recognition for the help he had given the Republic: the first time in November 1943, when he gave his word to the Germans that there were no Jews in San Marino; the second time when he helped Balducci convince Lieutenant Colonel Christiani not to raid Mount Titano. Instead of being awarded, he was kicked out of the country.

Ermenegildo Gasperoni, the veteran of the International Brigades in Spain, came out of hiding and officially founded the San Marino Communist Party. He finally received the just reward for the many risks he had taken, for the blows he had endured from the Fascists, and for the clandestine battles he had fought for the recognition of freedom of thought. He participated for decades in the San Marino political life at the highest ranks, although he was never a champion of good manners. In the 1980s, he went to China as a Captain Regent. At the official dinner, the waiters placed a finger bowl in front of each guest. Unaware that the water, containing a slice of lemon and a rose petal, was intended for washing hands, Gasperoni drank it. The members of the Chinese government did the same to avoid making him look bad.

After the war, Federico Bigi became Gasperoni's main political opponent. He was one of the founders of the San Marino Christian Democratic Party and engaged in intense activities while holding the highest institutional positions. In 1959, he was also appointed as the first President of the San Marino Olympic Committee. He concluded his long career as a Judge of the European Court of Human Rights in Strasbourg.

Alvaro Casali continued to work as a dentist and politician in the Socialist Party. In 1957, he strongly protested against the Soviet invasion of Hungary, and from that day forward, it can be said that his approach to public affairs became more moderate. He wrote several books about politics, which remain highly relevant today. He died in 1978, with a bullet still lodged near his heart.

Francesco Balsimelli continued his political involvement and teaching job at San Marino High School, where he became principal in 1958. He collaborated with many Italian and foreign newspapers and wrote historical, literary, and legal essays, as well as plays and musical fairy tales. Following his alleged affair with Regina Grymberg Brambilla, who returned to Milan, he was accused of having another romantic involvement, this time with a French teacher. He died on February 21, 1974. A few years later, Clara Boscaglia wrote about him: "... *It seemed to me that Francesco Balsimelli was the result of a reserved and protective world of San Marino that was not really inclined to imitate others; a world that produced its own original culture, if by culture we mean not only research and scholarship, but also creative abilities and an individual and collective way of life.*" In 2000, Edoardo Brambilla Grymberg proposed including Balsimelli in the list of the 'Righteous among the Nations,' but he did not provide sufficient evidence for the candidacy to be accepted.

Romano Michelotti, who risked his life numerous times in reckless motorcycle races during the war, dodging bombs to carry messages to various commands, founded the "San Marino Motorcycle Federation," which is now run by his son Amedeo.

Father Alfredo Cesari was appointed to lead the Commission for the Purge of Fascists from Public Offices by a law enacted on November 14, 1944, by the Great and General Council. He passed away on May 3, 1946, at the age of 53.

Alberto Marvelli, who had helped countless people and assisted numerous displaced persons in reaching Father Cesari's, was appointed as the head of the Commission for Accommodation by the Municipality of Rimini. He also sought to enter politics by joining the Christian Democrats. On the evening of October 5, 1946, Marvelli was struck and killed by an Allied military truck. Some reported that he was riding his bicycle to a political rally, while others claimed he was delivering aid to German soldiers residing in an enclave in the area of Bellaria. On September 5, 2004, he was declared Blessed.

CONCLUSIONS

Among the memories I collected about real or alleged Jews there are some which are real dilemmas. Yet, the stories told by the original inhabitants of San Marino are always so funny. For example, many people remembered a beautiful woman, whom everyone called "the Polish lady." She lived in the house owned by Marino Venturini, nicknamed "Gamben." This woman was also mentioned in Celio Gozi's memoirs, but at the end he corrected himself and wrote that she was not a Jew. In fact, I was able to verify that she did not live in San Marino during the period of the persecutions, but only a few years later. She was, in fact, an employee of the casino and rented Venturini's apartment in 1950.

Another noteworthy figure was a young man who was about 16 or 17 years old in 1944. Giorgio Zani vaguely remembered him, while Maria José Mandelli had very clear recollections of him. *"His name was Armando Movado, and he lived at the boarding school."* Therefore, as she affirmed, Father Cesari also put him up. Then she continued: *"He was shy and always sad; he said he was from Milan and that his father, the manufacturer of Movado watches, had died."*

After checking the information, I discovered that the last name "Movado" does not currently exist. However, even if it existed, it is well-known that Movado watches are not named after the owner of the company that produces them. The word comes from the Esperanto dictionary, published in the same year as the factory's foundation, and means "movement." That is why the manufacturer chose that name for his products. Who, then, was Armando Movado? In Bonfiglioli's case, it was clear that he used a fake name with common people, while he disclosed his real name to the Mandellis. Yet, Movado always kept his true identity to himself. One person told me that, in his opinion, that young man was actually Camillo De Benedetti, who was seen several times in San Marino after the war. But De Benedetti's widow assured me that her husband was in Switzerland during the war. It seems certain that the confusion originated from the fact that Father Cesari was housing another "Camillo," that is, "Camillo Castiglioni." So, who was "Armando Movado?" No one will probably ever know.

Another Polish woman is mentioned in local stories. This one had two children and lived at the beginning of Contrada Santa Croce, namely in the Jewish ghetto. There was also a family from Rome; they said their name was "Di Segni" and they were hidden at Paolo Sancisi's home. Sancisi was nicknamed "Paolino della Taverna" because, at that time, he was the owner of the restaurant "La Taverna."

Another family was hidden by the attorney Marino Michelotti, the last Fascist Captain Regent. Finally, there was also a family from Naples, named De Biagi, with two little girls. The nuns accommodated them at their tenant farmer's. They were in San Marino during the bombing on June 26, 1944. However, they were actually too far from their home, and their city had already been liberated by a local rebellion on October 1, 1943.

Of all the people described by Celio Gozi in his manuscript, there is one family he was certain was Jewish. The father, mother, and daughter all came from Prague. In this case, I will avoid publishing their names and merely say that the man began to trade in San Marino stamps. When I contacted the daughter, she was quite annoyed and denied her family's Jewish origin. She also asked me to let her father rest in peace.

But who was that man? He can be found twice in the State Archives. The first document is a note by Ezio Balducci, who used to record every suspicious action carried out by his sworn enemy,

Giuliano Gozi. On an undated sheet of paper, Balducci wrote that "Giuliano Gozi" had set up an illegal trade of San Marino stamps and coins with a displaced person and that man might have been either "a Jew or an international spy." It is clear that Balducci was referring to this man. In fact, he left San Marino after the war due to an allegation of fraud against the Philatelic Office. However, Balducci also suspected that he was a "spy"! What was Balducci referring to? There was a copy of an interrogation, a few documents after this paper, carried out by Political Inspector Pietro Animali concerning the arrests at the Cemetery of Montalbo. Following that ambush, Gasperoni had been imprisoned, and the Anti-Fascists from Rimini had been dragged to the SS command to be executed. Some printed leaflets were found during the arrest. The man confessed to the Inspector that he had lent the typewriter and the printing machine to Luigi Giancecchi and Ermenegildo Gasperoni. Therefore, we can assume that they immediately realized who had informed the "Black Shirts and the SS" about their meeting place! The accusation of fraud also pertains to the printing machine owned by this man: many believed that he used it to print fake stamps of San Marino.

Now what remains to be decided is whether this person was a Jew or not. Mrs. Lenka Matusicova, head of the department of the archives at the Jewish Museum in Prague, stated that this man was not found in the archives of the people belonging to the Jewish community, and that nothing about him was even found in the city's Civil Registry. So, who was he? And why was he suspected to be Jewish? Did he pretend to be a Jew because Jewish people were treated better in San Marino? Or was he really a spy whose mission was to infiltrate the territory of San Marino as a Jew? If so, this fact would also explain the Germans' requests not to house members of the Jewish race.

The question I have been asked in recent times is always the same: "How many Jews sought refuge in San Marino?" For various reasons, including the lack of time needed to carry out thorough research, I was only able to analyze in detail the area of the old town center of San Marino, where I could ascertain the presence of sixty-two people, among whom were Jews and individuals married to Jews. However, there are also traces of the alleged presence of Jews in other parts of the Republic. A reliable source reported various baptisms administered to both adults and children by the priest, Don Settimio Nicolini, in the parish of Acquaviva. This seems to have occurred during the period immediately after the proclamation of the Racial Laws in Italy, but I was not permitted to view the parish archives. The priest's noble gesture of helping out must be recognized, but it should also be pointed out that this practice was almost immediately made worthless due to the continuous changes to the Racial Laws. At first, they established conversions had to occur before March 1919, except for those who were born after that date. The next restrictive modification, which rendered baptisms of convenience entirely ineffective, was the amendment of the regulations regarding the so-called "Demorazza" (Demography and Race). From then on, those who wanted to avoid having their documents stamped with the words "belonging to the Jewish race" had to submit their certificate of baptism, along with those of their parents and grandparents. So, and I would also add unfortunately, Don Settimio's efforts were worthless.

In Montegiardino, the teacher Alceste Preda Ferri claimed she had Jewish children among her pupils during the war. They were shy and reserved and sat at the back of the class. Professor Fernando Bindi told me that Bruno Casalgrandi and his daughter, both from Castelvetro in Modena, lived in his house in Acquaviva.

In Borgo Maggiore, the Faenza family from Milan was hosted by the Martellis.

In other places, some people gave the Jews the documents of their relatives who had emigrated abroad, pretending they had repatriated.

In the chaos of the last period of the war, everyone could be hidden. Every house gave shelter to dozens of refugees, and the twelve train tunnels were packed tight. In the last period of the Second World War, there were seven displaced people for each citizen, including children. Regarding the children, a story which deeply moved me is the one told by Lina Giannini, a woman in her nineties from Serravalle. She put up eighty-three people in her house, twenty-two of them were children: *"Adults did not need much. I made them some piadina*[185] *and vegetables, but the children had to eat some meat. So, at night I went to steal chickens; well, not really steal them: nearby there were families who had taken refuge in the tunnels and had abandoned all their courtyard animals at home... At night I occasionally went to get a hen... but I only gave the meat to the children... there were twenty-two of them. Then I brought home an old woman whose son wanted to throw her off a nearby bridge to stop her from suffering... I took her to my house... I said to myself: I'm already taking care of so many people; one more won't make much difference."*

I asked her whether she had ever put up any Jews and she candidly replied: *"No, I never housed Jews... But I did host Germans."*

"What type of Germans? Were they soldiers?" *"Nooo... tourists!"*

"Tourists? In that period?" *"It was the time of the bombing and my friend, Ezio Balducci brought them to my home. He told me that he had stopped them in Borgo Maggiore. They wanted to go and visit the old town center, but it was impossible because there were bombs falling up there, so he took them to my house instead. They were families... they stayed here for the whole summer. They did not speak a word of Italian."*

"Did they tell you their names?" *"No, none of them ever told me his name. After the war they all went away."*

"Did they give you any money for the hospitality?" *"No, I did not take anything from any of the people I put up... However, a few years later I went with a neighbor of mine to the fair in Santarcangelo where a man recognized me. He started to scream... this woman saved my life! This woman saved me! I must say I was quite embarrassed with that man shouting in the middle of all those people... He gave me a lot of stuff. We came home with the car full of every sort of thing. That was the only time someone had ever given me anything."*

Lina Giannini's words make me think about that first question: How many Jews took refuge in San Marino? During the most crucial

185. Flat unleavened type of bread. [translator's note].

period of World War II, how many of them could actually have been hidden in a country where some people believed that German families could go to the forefront as tourists?

"*Many!*" replied Adelia Cesari, "many." Father Alfredo Cesari's favorite niece had still another surprise for me. His family members were landowners. They had several farms both in San Marino and in areas close to the border.

"My uncle Alfredo hid many Jews in the Convent, but most of them were housed in our farms! He gave them all fake documents, dressed them as peasants and made them work in the fields."

"But where did he keep them hidden?" *"Everywhere. In his brothers' houses, at the farmers' who rented other farmlands... The largest group was put up at the Bonfé family's house, on our farm between Domagnano and Valdragone."*

"Do you mean in Corianino?" *"That's right, I think that's the name of that area."*

"But how many Jews did Father Cesari hide?" *"Oh... more than a hundred!"*

Then, if Father Cesari alone was able to hide more than one hundred Jews, how many were there all together? It can be seen from the witnesses' memories that these persecuted people were evenly scattered throughout the territory. In most cases, they were perfectly hidden and, as Celio Gozi wrote: *"In some cases, not even the owners of the houses where they were living knew their true identity."*

Thanks also to Gozi's manuscript, I can now count sixty-two people just in the old town center, but I guess there could have actually been at least twice as many of them, or maybe even more! We can guess that if we multiply these individuals by the municipalities which the Republic of San Marino is divided up into, the total number could equal over 1,000 people! This, again, is just a hypothesis, but I am willing to bet on it.

Today I have come back to the Mandellis' house. At first glance it seems that everything has remained as it was then: the shutters, as well as the front door, are dried out and stripped of paint by time. An old, rusted, wrought iron gate gives access to the rear part of the house, where the small shelter was dug into the rock, but someone has removed the mountain stone to turn the place into a small courtyard. On the side of the house, you can still see the traces of a walled-up door. It must have been the side door from where the eight children used to come out during that frightening autumn of 1943.

Then, I moved onto the road and looked back at the path described by Maria José Mandelli, "*We walked hand in hand towards Attorney Balsimelli's house.*" Today, "Pandemonium" Attilio Balsimelli's house is a bank, but at the bottom, resting on the sidewalk, you can still see the two small windows of the cellar where those innocent, terrified children were hiding and looking through the slit at the shoes of the people passing by.

So, I began to think: Why has nobody ever told this story before? Why has all this time gone by? I quickly recollected my thoughts on the event. Ezio Balducci and the Republican Fascist Government, which was not Fascist at all, did protect the Jews, but received almost all of them as an inheritance! A great majority of them were already here when the Fascists took action! The Jews had arrived during the domination of the Gozis, who definitely behaved like dictators, but left the Jews alone! In compliance with the most ancient local traditions, in which the Republic of San Marino had housed and protected persecuted people from every part of the world very often in the past, citizens of San Marino acted in the same way, as if hospitality were written in their genetic code: "Relinquo vos liberos ab utroque homine". According to legend, these are the last words spoken by Saint Marinus to his community: "I leave you free from all the other men." These words became part of the DNA of this community thanks to its Holy founder. Since then, they seem to have been passed down for centuries, flowing in the veins of the people who have lived on this three-peaked rock. In that historical period, the "other men" must have been the Nazis. Nobody had to or wanted to rehabilitate the Fascists in San Marino! They were responsible for every bad action they carried out, but not for this one! Thus, quoting an old motto, the baby was thrown out with the bathwater.

Yet history took its course. It was difficult to find Maria José Mandelli. First of all, I knew her only by her nickname, "Baby." She was the most reliable direct witness I could find: a young girl at the time, she was the person most aware of what was going on. The first time I was able to talk to her on the phone, she sounded reluctant, almost annoyed that I was trying to awaken so many terrible memories. During my second call, I wanted to ask her if she would consent to being interviewed, but she did not give me the chance to do so. She began shooting off the names of her old friends, almost like a machine gun. She wanted information about all of them: how were Giorgio, Gina, Giovanni and his brothers, and many others. In my third phone call, I immediately interrupted her and said: "Some think that the people in San Marino took advantage of the situation or of your family, for example. It is also said that some people made money off the Jews. Is this true?" She replied with her gentle yet firm voice: *"No! They treated us all very well!"* Then, without giving her time to change the subject and start asking questions again about her old friends, I said: "Can I come to Reggio Calabria and interview you?" She started to sob and whispered, *"You know, I'm quite relieved now because I wanted to ask you the same thing. Last night, I spoke to my son. We discussed it together, and I concluded that it is high time the world is told this story!"*

Celio Gozi was right: "The Fascist Republic of San Marino was the only country in Europe and the only state controlled by the Axis which had the audacity to give shelter and protect the Jews during World War II." Of course, he made errors about some names. For example, he referred to the Grünfelds as "Grinfelds," as he heard their names being pronounced, and he mistakenly identified Edoardo Brambilla as a girl. Yet, he wrote what he saw and heard, and that was true, all true, as the clearly falsified documents at the Registry Office demonstrate. There was a political will behind those actions, a clearly studied strategy according to which "all human beings are equal in San Marino and should be treated as such." This is the reason why the citizens of San Marino suffered from starvation to help feed the flood of refugees and risked their lives to hide so many Jews. Of course, many in San Marino were unaware of the presence of the Jews, but many others were not. Several knew they were there, though they did not know who they were, while many others knew them very well and protected them at the risk of their own lives!

Today, the witnesses' recollections are often joyful and funny, but they represent the memories of the survivors — those who made it, those who glanced up and saw the war around the corner. They are the memories of the children who crossed from one side of Italy to the other, believing that their continual migration was due to the cold weather. Now, they all agree on one thing: they are part of a story, and this story must be told, capturing both its sweet and bitter nuances.

In the speech delivered during the celebrations for the tenth anniversary of the end of the war, Alvaro Casali spoke words that seemed to have foretold this story. He knew the whole truth but did not relay it. Perhaps the world was not ready for it yet. He finished his speech by saying: "These brief concise notes I wanted to include to remind you of an unfortunate and perhaps isolated period in the century-old history of the Republic of San Marino, will one day be of help to those who want to write a more detailed and documented description of these terrible events that will remain in the annals of this millenary Republic." Although he was the first person to notice that Camillo Castiglioni was not a monk and became his close friend, Casali did not mention anything about him or the others at that time. Yet, he announced that someone would eventually do it.

It might have been his hand that guided my own today! I looked for passports that I had never found throughout the years, so I saw complete failure before my eyes. Today, however, I realized something much more important. Before leaving, I took one last look at that window facing the sidewalk. A long line of big trees has replaced the flowers along Viale Antonio Onofri. There is no longer any trace of the thorny bushes. Yet, if you close your eyes, you can still smell the roses.

www.ingramcontent.com/pod-product-compliance
Lightning Source LLC
LaVergne TN
LVHW010057110826
845155LV00028B/375

* 9 7 8 1 9 4 8 6 5 1 7 3 8 *